A Man's Guide to
Getting it Wrong

By Craig Jones and Siôn James

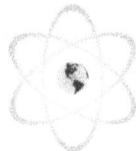

2016, TWB Press
www.twbpress.com

A Man's Guide to Getting it Wrong
Copyright © 2016 by Craig Jones & Siôn James

Edited by Terry Wright

© Cover Art by Craig Jones & Siôn James

ISBN: 978-1-944045-13-5

Men and women... we're different, you know.

It is a truth universally acknowledged that a man in possession of a good relationship must be in want of screwing it up royally.

Now I'm not talking about the scumbags, the sleazebags, the bullies or the drunks. I'm talking about the man fully committed to his wife or girlfriend, the one before all else that he puts first, the person that, dare I say it, he actually admits to his mates down at the pub that he 'loves'. He's attracted her interest, he's pursued her, he's managed to convince her that he's worth bothering with, and then, in a very un-laddish display of affection, he mans up and commits.

The outcome: shock horror, he's happy. More importantly, *she* is happy. Everyone around them looks in on their relationship and comments on how perfect everything seems to be. They giggle, they openly concur with their cohort, and to the outside world they are this flaming beacon of hope that love truly does exist, that love in fact conquers all.

Bullshit! Because behind closed doors, away from the jealous eyes of loveless friends, there is no doubt that the very things that have him rolling around on the floor and gasping for breath, once toned and smooth stomach muscles cramping with laughter, are the same things that have her flexing her index finger and calling him into the kitchen 'to have a word.' And although he will stand like a scolded schoolboy, head down, fingers respectfully laced behind his back, agreeing that this is not the behaviour of a grown up, he is secretly already thinking of the next time. And how the next time he'll make sure that he doesn't get caught. And how the next time, wouldn't it be great if his mates did it too?

Now if you are a woman reading this and your first thought was "Well (insert name here) used to be like that but not anymore, he's grown into this blah blah blah..." then the first thing you need to realise is that you are wrong. Not in the 'you think you know the offside rule' type of wrong, but in a 'you are kidding yourself beyond all belief' kind of wrong. He may be hiding it well. It may not have surfaced in a number of years but trust me, it lays dormant, watching and waiting, and no matter how much you try to convince yourself, it will return and it will ruin all of his good work in about thirty seconds flat.

Because while he is the very definition of good now, the truth is that he's faking it. You know, like you used to when you could be bothered.

And if you're a man reading this and you genuinely believe that you've changed, that you took part in your last drinking game when you stopped playing rugby, that, of course, you leave the room to fart, and that you don't only know what the toilet brush is for but actually use it, then I don't need to tell you who is the liar, liar pants on fire. It's you, and you know it. Because you are more than aware that it lurks, under the radar, but lurking all the same, and all it will take is a trigger, like the subconscious key word left in the mind of the hypnotist's stooge, to bring your laddish behaviour back with a bang.

You're both shaking your head, aren't you? Man and woman alike, disagreeing with me but agreeing with each other until the cows come home. Maybe you make the most of your 'special time' and read together, and as you've progressed, you've given each other a little smile that says, "Hey, he's talking about everybody else, everybody except for us." Maybe you're crowded around, and how cute is this, your *shared* Kindle, loaded full of chick-lit and the classics and not a single Chris Ryan or Stephen King in sight, mutually loving the groundbreaking *wireless way to read a book* (which by the way *is* a fucking book and always has been), with smug arrogance. Smug arrogance because this just isn't you anymore, right?

Wrong!

Wrong, and I can prove it.

Let's take, umm, we'll call them Drew and Jane. Okay, so their real names are not Drew and Jane, you probably worked that out, but I'm going to be in enough trouble as it is when I say, "Hey, have you read my book," and there they are, smack bang in the opening chapter. Because when the bloke screws things up, it is usually in a way that has the knack of sticking in the memory. Especially the woman's memory. While Drew may have forgotten what put him in the doghouse, trust me when I say that Jane, even today, has still got a hold on the leash, ready and waiting for the next time her man needs to be muzzled. And the reason that what Drew did sticks in Jane's memory, of course, is that he had been 'good' for a very long time. Years, in fact. He'd been so level-headed that his mother-in-law could have come on his stag do. On the other hand, asking said mother-in-law at the subsequent wedding if she'd been the stripper at said bachelor party was a question that got another friend in so much trouble...but that is a whole other story.

A Man's Guide to Getting it Wrong

After University, Drew and Jane got married and moved away and he didn't see his mates so much. Time passed and although they kept in touch through email and text messages (because blokes will *never* talk to each other on the phone if they can help it) no one seemed to have the time to meet up. Jane stepped in, insisted he invite his two best friends, also now both married, and their spouses for a weekend. Maybe it's best if I let Drew tell you where it all went wrong.

Drew, 32, Chartered Accountant. Bedford.

"Things couldn't have been going better. Jane was playing the hostess role like no one else does, you know, and Neil and Dan's wives knew each other anyway, so we were set. Friday night we went out, had a curry, a few beers, and to be honest, the lot of us were shattered, you know, after a week of work and, of course, those guys had travelled. Saturday was when it got messy. The girls wanted to go shopping, but there was rugby on and a fridge full of beer that we hadn't even started on the night before, you know, so it didn't take too long to convince the girls that we'd only mess up their shopping trip. Four hours later and two trips to the off licence and we were well oiled, but not out of order. It's not like we left the toilet seat up, you know. So the girls come back and they've really bonded and they're happy to order in takeout. After dinner, me and the boys, we tidy up, do the dishes, you know, and the girls crack open, I don't know, a second, maybe third bottle of wine and stick on a *Take That* CD. So they're in the lounge, we're in the kitchen when Neil reminds us of what we used to do at Uni. "Come on," he says, "We've not done it for years... let's do the Naked Run!" Now a Naked Run isn't really, you know, like fully naked. You still wear your underpants. But you've got to leg it around the block, whooping and occasionally flashing your arse. Now, you know, if he'd said that an hour before or an hour afterwards, me and Dan wouldn't have been up for it, but as the girls belted out 'Never Forget' from behind the closed living room door, the opportunity, you know, it was just there. So we strip down to our boxer shorts, or in the case of Dan these freaky little tight things that just dragged your eye to his area, you know, and creep out from the kitchen to the hallway, giggling like we were reliving our primary school days, not Uni, sucking our guts in like we've still got a Jonny Bravo six pack hidden in there someplace, and it's at that moment, as we're pulling on our shoes, that the music goes off and the lounge door swings open."

Dan has to stop here for a few minutes. Tears are rolling down his face.

"Sorry, sorry. They just stood there, you know. Staring at us. Then Neil bursts out laughing and Jane brushes past me without making eye contact. She's got this look on her face like I've shat on her dad's car. "A word," she says. "In the kitchen." She stands in the doorway, and for some reason, I'm still trying to pull on my shoes, and then up go her eyebrows into this arch that seriously terrified me, so I moved my butt into that kitchen, you know, like as fast as I could. Our visitors were gone by nine the next morning and they've not been back since. I still don't see what all the fuss was about."

Jane's version of the story is more sombre. It

takes more effort, and coercing, to drag the words out of her. It's a painful process, like she's having a wisdom tooth pulled without any anaesthetic. Whereas Drew was somewhat proud that he and his friends could rewind the clock so quickly, take up from just where they had left off, Jane simply does not see the point of why they would want to regress in the first place.

Jane, 30, Primary School Teacher, Bedford.

"So they just stand there, moronic grins on their faces like they're a couple of kids from my class caught telling a dirty joke, next to naked in the hall. It's not like any of them is a bloody Adonis either. Yes, they all played a lot of sport when they were younger, but good God, they're not exactly holding off middle aged spread. And the three of them were going to inflict *that* on the neighbours! It was half past eight in the evening. Children would have seen them. One of them had, well, piss stains on his pants! Okay, it was Drew! Drew had bloody piss stains right there, on display! I was mortified. Drew had never, and I mean never, done anything like that before. Or so I thought. Turns out half of Cardiff had seen their bloody

'Naked Run' during the three years they'd studied there. "It's a laugh!" That was his excuse. "It's a laugh!" For who? Not for me, I'll tell you that. And I'll tell you something else. He won't be bloody doing it again!"

After his friends left, Drew spent three nights in the spare room and another month deeply committed to some serious sucking up. If he is honest, which I am not in the least bit suggesting he was when we spoke alone, with Jane nowhere in earshot, he is still not sure what he did wrong.

And therein lies the problem. The things the man does to land himself in hot water, in the doghouse, or at least on the path to royally screwing up his relationship with the love of his life are not intentional, or vindictive or malicious. It's not like Drew was found in a compromising situation with a friend's wife or was caught knocking one out to Babe Station. It is simply by being a man that a man gets himself into the bad books.

And now you, the happy couple reading this together by the romantic backlight of your Kindle, are both nodding again but this time for totally different reasons, aren't you? Wife or girlfriend, nodding because all those things that wound you up, the ones he called trivial, have come pouring back into your memory, changing those loving glances into a cold hard stare. And all the while, husband/ boyfriend is nodding too, thinking that there's so many things worse than a Naked Run.

A Fool and His Penis.

Let's face one certain fact together, shall we? Without a doubt the one part of the man that will lead him into temptation and will not deliver him from evil is his penis. Now, as I've said, we're not talking about the down and dirty love rat, 'my penis is a divining rod searching out a little bit of strange' type of bloke, so get that thought out of your mind right away. We're talking about the righteous man. We're talking about the type of man you'd want your sister to be dating. Maybe, if she had to date anyone at all, ever. We're talking about the type of man who, when he is not with the love of his life, does not even see his penis as a thing of sexual pleasure, for him or for anybody else. We are talking about the type of man who sees his penis as the greatest thing he has had to play with since his first Subbuteo set, and, as a bonus, tucked in there right next to it in their own bespoke bag, he's got a very special set of marbles to fool around with too.

So all the men will be asking, where's the harm in having a bit of a rummage, a subtle readjustment or stretching it out to see how long it *really* is? And this is where the problems start, because while the women are shaking their heads right now, all the men will be shrugging. "So what?" they'll be saying. "It's not like I'm doing anything wrong," they'll believe. "It's not like I'm rubbing up against the leg of some early twenties bimbette and giving her the dry-hump of her life." They'll grin cheekily. And even though they may well be right, as far as the woman in their life is concerned, they could not be further off the mark if the mark was the South Pole and they were happily having a fiddle with their North Pole!

Because when it comes to getting it wrong, most women would agree that men, no matter what their age, should not be using their penis as a toy. Well, at least not in public. There is a time and a place for such behaviour, apparently. Having a quiet grope to make ourselves comfortable is frowned upon. Being unaware that a video camera is rolling is not an excuse for getting caught on film; keeping the little fella warm on a cold and frosty day is not a defence. In fact, I would go as far as to suggest that any video evidence of penis playing is pretty much taboo. But there is much worse that a man can and, of course, does decide to do to his closest friend. Like hiding it. Men, you see, are inherently jealous of women. Very jealous, in fact. It's mainly because the ladies have all of the things that men are most interested. Think lady parts, north and south, and you've got it. How many men have said that if they had boobies then they'd never leave the house? Now many of today's so called modern men are developing their own set of man boobs. Is trying to achieve the aesthetic of the vagina ever going to do a man any good? As we are to find out, the answer is a resounding 'no'. What is even more worrying is that such behaviour is not the worst of it. Only a man can spend time in the mirror imagining that his 'weapon' of choice is a light sabre and wield it like a Jedi. And boys, please be aware that why you may think your virile erection is in fact a compliment to the beauty and sexual phenomena that is your loved one, she is not going to take too kindly if you get aroused for all around to see. So where to start when there are so many ways a man can get it wrong? Well, we have to start somewhere, so are you sitting comfortably? Then we'll begin.

Gloria, 68, Retired, Swansea.

"Now the thing was that I'd been asking him for years, like, to take me to the theatre, and when out of the blue, he buys us these tickets, I was landed. So off we go, down to the

Grand, all dressed up, Shakespeare see. Gorgeous it was, Romeo and Juliet, so romantic. And I'm feeling even better, like, because there's no way Jim would have wanted to come to something like this yet he's done it for me, so I look across at him, all handsome, clean shaved in his best suit, legs wide open, playing *at himself*, like he had a lump of putty down there! He wasn't even trying to hide it. He didn't even stick his hand in his pocket. No, right there for all to see. Said he was putting himself 'tidy,' he did. Trust me, he's not been 'tidy' down there for years. Said he wasn't comfy. So I ask him why he doesn't just go to the toilet, like, and he says it was only for a second and he doesn't get that it just wasn't appropriate."

It would appear that 'appropriateness' is a continual bone of discontent, a running theme that men do not necessarily fully understand. If asked, a woman would say that the penis has its place... Okay, let me stop you there. Who grinned when they read that line? I know you're not meant to laugh at your own wit, but I couldn't help myself on that one. Sorry, ladies, I'm sure my lack of focus is annoying; I'll try harder to keep on task. Right...where was I? Ah, yes. If asked, a woman would say that the penis has its place, hidden until the time is right for it to make its guest appearance. The thing is, girls, what you don't understand is that a penis is like an Xbox. You do not realise how much fun it can be unless you have one of your own.

Honestly, there's just so much you can do with it, flaccid or flag poled. Every man in the world has stretched his out to see how far it will reach. Fact. Any man who says he has never done that is lying. By the way, any woman who has seen a man treat his cock like an elastic band and hasn't wished it would stay that length for longer is also lying. Now if you're not some sex addict, it's likely your old boy will stay deflated more than it's inflated, but such sagging should never be a barrier to self fun. With so much 'looseness' to mess around with, it's just a minefield down there, as in, it's mine and it's getting feeled! It can be twisted, doubled over, even hidden away by pulling the excess elbow skin of the scrotum up and over it. And being an undercover lover of one's own genitalia does not need to be an indoor activity.

Pete, 35, Rugby Club Stalwart, Pontypool.

"During a rugby presentation night, our coach was talking about the difference between forwards and backs. To illustrate his point he dimmed the lights and played some footage from a winter's game, caught on camera. During an injury to one of the opposition players, our forwards are bound in a huddle, steam rising from them as Gibbo, our captain and prop, verbally rips them to shreds over something. The camera pans out and captures pretty much all the backs, lined up in attacking formation, each and every one of us groping ourselves. It was very funny."

The options and, dare I say it, opportunities, when indoors though are endless. Why play pocket billiards when in the comfort of your own home you can just lob it out and twang away? It's like the difference between watching sport on the telly or actually being there at the stadium. It would appear however that our partners would rather we retired from this particular sport, at least while they are in the room and therefore potential spectators, but while the occasional juggle may not result in the red card being administered, it is important to work out where the line between a bookable offence and an early bath sits.

Dave found out the hard way.

Dave, 29, Insurance Adjuster, Leicester.

"Okay, so I admit that it probably wasn't the wisest move ever but it was just a bit of fun. You've seen Silence of the Lambs, yeah? The bit where the other serial killer, Buffalo Bill or something, is dancing in front of the camera? He's collecting women's skin, making a coat or whatever from it, and he's wearing it and then he tucks his, you know, his, umm... bits between his legs so he looks like a girl. Right, you've seen it, yeah? I can tell, cos that's the look every bloke that's watched that film gets when you talk about that scene, cos we've all done it. We've all tucked it away just to see what we'd look like. My mate said he used to whip it in and out while chanting 'Man... Woman'. Got banned from his local, he did. Man, you've done it. I can tell. And alright, most blokes don't stand there waiting for their girlfriend to get out of the shower with their cock and balls shoved between their thighs to ask them if they look like a pretty little girl, but I was messing about, having a laugh. I thought she'd find it funny. She went ballistic. I thought she'd over-reacted to be honest, but I guess not. Next time I did it, she dumped me!"

Dave's former girlfriend, Susan, was not in the slightest bit impressed by Dave's puerile and penile magicianship. It wasn't so much that he thought it was the funniest thing he'd ever done but that he didn't learn from her first reaction not to be such a cock-hider again.

Susan, 29, Insurance Adjuster, Northampton.

"We'd met in work and I thought he was different, if I'm honest. I'd been with the Jack-the-Lad types before, and Dave just seemed, well like I said, different. So a few months in and I'm thinking, yeah, this is going somewhere, and just then it seemed like he turned into this complete idiot. It's like he regressed back to childhood. Well, not that far back. Like to being a teenager realising he had something between his legs for the first time. He was obsessed with it. Scratching it. Messing with it. But when he did the 'being a girl' thing..."

Susan pulls a face like she's licking piss off a nettle as she stands up, squeezing her thighs together to illustrate exactly what she means.

"So I told him off. We had a bit of a row but he seemed genuinely sorry. A couple of weeks later we're in bed, kissing and stuff, and I go to put my hand... *there*... and the sick shit has only done it again. Tucked it away between his legs and I'm feeling like I'm touching up another woman and he's pissing himself laughing. God it makes me so mad to think of it now, but at the time I went fucking nuts. Kicked him out of my flat, and the next day I decided enough was enough. But even seeing him in work after that was odd. Like I knew he had a dirty, twisted secret. Which, you know what, he has! In the end I asked for a transfer. I couldn't bear to look at him."

The most difficult incidences to deal with of course become manifest when you're least expecting them. And when this happens, it may not always be your wife or girlfriend who are the ones to pass comment. And judgement. Sometimes it's even worse. Much worse.

Sean, 34, Public Health Practitioner, Brighton.

"I'd gone round to my mum's for dinner after work and we're sat there, watching a bit of TV. I got myself in a right comfortable position, kind of dozing a bit, and without taking her eyes off the telly my mum asks, dead casual, "Lost him, have you?" and I realise I've got one hand down the front of my trousers, nice and warm, and perfectly reflected in the television screen. I'll tell you, it was worse being caught like that as an adult than it was being caught with a porno mag as a kid. Six months it took me to go back there for dinner."

You've noticed, I hope, that I've tried to avoid situations of a sexual nature because that would simply be too easy. We, as men, know we get it wrong in the bedroom on occasion, but we also hope that we get it right a greater proportion of the time. If not, tell us. We follow instruction well. Now, we've all been caught 'being intimate' with ourselves at some stage in our lives, and if truth be known, there's nothing wrong with that. It's healthy, invigorating and satisfying. And it doesn't truly get us in the really bad books, but an erect penis *is* like a little incendiary device likely to go off at any moment. Please remember that using your swollen member as a plaything is a direct gateway to getting it wrong.

Who hasn't been tempted to use the Little General (or whatever other personal name you may have for your one-eyed womb warrior) as a truncheon? Even during moments of pleasure, men the world over have considered 'smurfing' their loved one on the top of the head with their engorged phallus. Men are proud of their erections. Whereas women most probably think of them as ugly looking things that occasionally get the job done, men see them as an extension of their machismo, there to be glorified, to be worshipped, something to be waved around in the air. This is not an approach that many women find attractive, as Gary discovered to his cost.

Gary, 24, Decorator, Liverpool.

"Mate, it was mental how I got dumped. We're back at her place, on the settee, proper going for it and she says I should go and wait for her in the bedroom. Well, fuck me, I didn't need to be told twice mate, so while she nips to the loo I gets in there and gets proper bollocko. So I'm stood there and she's got this full length mirror and I'm checking myself out, this proper stiffy sticking out in front of me, so I grabs hold of it with two hands, right down by my nuts, and I'm swinging it from side to side, making noises like it's a light sabre from Star Wars. And just as I'm saying the famous line she walks in and she doesn't catch the first bit, just the second bit and she flips out and now she won't even answer the phone to me."

Gary shakes his head. All his energy has gone and he looks a bit lost. I ask him what quote he was half way through when his girlfriend had walked in to find him holding his erect penis like a light sabre. He sighs. He can't look me in the eye and he drops his gaze to his trainers. He is virtually whispering when he starts to talk again.

"Ah, mate, it's embarrassing. I was doing my best Darth Vader voice and I'd said, 'Luuuuke', and then I swung it around and the door opened and she's staring straight at it, and it's staring straight back at her and then the rest of the quote comes out. 'I am your father'. I couldn't help it. The words just came out. Fuck me, no wonder I'm single."

There will come the time of course that even

when the penis will behave exactly as it should, it will still get you in trouble. The thing is that the penis is very prehistoric in nature. Stimulus. Response. If you wave a raw steak in the face of a crocodile, then you know what's going to happen, right? Well, the penis is just the same. So maybe when the poor man is in the bad books, maybe, just maybe, on occasion, it is not the man's fault. Maybe, just maybe, on occasion, it is actually down to our better halves.

Penny, 31, Chef, Bath.

"So we're going to this fancy dress party on a boat for our friend, Frasier, and we all have to dress up as pirates because he had a pirate party for his fifth birthday. Now Jason has been mates with Frasier for years and has seen a photo from that party where one of the kids didn't come as a pirate but came as Superman, so Jason decides that's what he wants to go as. It was really funny, and Frasier got it, even if some of the others didn't. The outfit was pretty tight and it had all these fake muscles built in, and I won't lie to you, Jason looked the part. Anyway, the night progresses and we have a few beers and all I do is reach up and kiss him on the ear, and suddenly he goes bright red and covers himself with his cape. I ask him what he's playing at so he gingerly moves the cape aside, and in his super tight superman pants he's got a boner like a teenager. Next thing you know there are camera flashes going off, and he's not even attempting to hide it anymore. Seriously. He's thirty-five next birthday. Does he have no control? Jeez, he even tried to tell me I should take it as a compliment. Well, I'll tell you, there's a time and a place for *that* type of compliment!"

Jason, 34, Bar Manager, Bath.
"Hahahahahahahahahahahahahahah ahahaha! Sorry. Hahahahahaha!"

So whenever you ask yourself the question "What did I do wrong?" think of the one place that you should never actually think *with*, because that shake of the head, that wag of the finger or that sudden empty and cold space in the bed next to you may have come from a scratch, a grope or a swing of that troublemaking mate of yours, your penis. Because he is *not* an appropriate plaything, no matter how much you love him, hard or soft.

Memoir of a Geezer

It's about time, I believe, that we meet our eponymous hero, the Everyman guaranteed to get it wrong at each and every turn. Everyone knows a Geezer, defined by his way with both the words and the ladies, but what makes our Geezer different is his ability to take a seemingly winning situation and drag from it a humiliating defeat. But don't take my word for it. Take his!

Making the good impression...well, at least trying too!

"Okay, so you've successfully negotiated the run up and you're in your stride, having cleared the first and second hurdle of the evening: those being the eyeballing treatment and the pleasantries. Come on! You can do this! You know you can!

The eyeballing treatment was a taller than expected hurdle. Rosie, my girlfriend (and fiancé aka wife to be) had sunk into one of the big brown leather sofas in the restaurant's main window, when a taxi pulled up directly next to where we had sat. From the corner of my eye, there was a mass of blurred movement through beaming lights and a burrowing into the side of my head. Nerves had sat Rosie up straight.

"They're here," she whispered through her teeth as if she was a ventriloquist. She smiled but my bum began to sweat. I turned and looked through the window. The blurring in the corner of my eye had been many pairs of hands waving from, not a taxi, but a *minibus*. I squinted out through the glass just as my rectum became a swimming pool of perspiration. There were hoards of them out there. The beaming lights were racks of many teeth in wide smiles, and the burrowing into my head were the busy eyes of Rosie's family (my future in-laws to be). I instantly did that looking cool act, that "ha ha" laugh that people do when they are nervous and try to deflect their anxieties or at least mask them. So I "ha ha'd," turned around to carry on the pretend jovial conversation only to realise Rosie, my girlfriend (and fiancé aka wife to be), wasn't even there! I had pretend laughed back into my seat with a pretend joke from the Invisible Man.

I quickly turned back to the full length window to see my future in-laws lined up like the bad guys in

The Usual Suspects. I waited to hear a voice asking me to identify the person who was *going* to mug me! I'd have answered 'all of them!' I pulled my belly-hugging sweatshirt away from my stomach to mask the early onset of my middle age girth at 25, managed a somewhat nervous smile (this time looking like someone famous from the movies: Hannibal Lecter) and a lifted my hand in nervous acknowledgement. Can't say I cleared hurdle one with any confidence, especially if they saw me laughing and commenting in reply to the nobody next to me. Yet, to this day it has never been mentioned, so whether I cleared it, or possibly just ran through it, I'll leave up to you to judge. I greet them with a jovial "Hello, I'm xxxx."

Hurdle two was cleared with no more than a slight graze to the inside of my ankle when my potential – and in this case – future Nana-in-law asked me to repeat myself. I was nervous. I could feel my words fluttering off on the backs of butterflies that were escaping my stomach. I managed to jerk off the slight embarrassment with a clearing of my throat, and again strung the few words together. This time I attempted to dampen the accent with which my vocal chords coated the sentence. It was to no avail. I almost managed to repeat myself word perfect, accent free and could feel the tension slipping out of my back and shoulders as I neared the end when, with just a few words remaining...

"I can't understand a word *he's* saying," Nana-in-law-to-be proclaimed to the whole lot of them on 'Meet the Family (In-Laws to be) Night'. I laughed off the awkwardness in keeping with the sniggers of those who had come to see if their daughter's, their sister's, their grand-daughter's fuss was really merited. As I've said, I took a slight graze to the ankle in clearing the second hurdle. The conversation moved on, leaving poor Nana-in-law-to-be in a confused and lonely void where the conversation went astray, over her head even, and I felt my confidence surge. I could do this. I could...

But wait...I look up and all I can see are more hurdles coming. Even as we sat down to dinner they were approaching with haste and with little distance between them. I could see them as plain as you see these words on this page. The elder I'd come to know as Granddad the Great was wiggling his finger at me from the top end of the table, where all heads of the family sit, especially ones with a name like Granddad the Great. I'd slipped into another movie it seemed: the Godfather! Nana-in-law-to-be was staring blankly at me from the opposite side of the table, muttering to herself, trying to work out if I'm 'one of those illegal immigrants with an accent like that.' My father-in-law-to-be was reaching for my name somewhere in his box of vocabulary but the words were playing hide 'n' seek. When he caught hold of them, he'd look up and catch his breath. Then the name slipped his grasp, and he disengaged. Worse was that my girlfriend was in full-blown conversation with her sister...and her back was turned to me!

I felt exposed, vulnerable, like a knight without his shield on the battlefield to deflect spears of inappropriateness. And there just had to be one of those coming, didn't there, surely it was inevitable I was going to be skewed by one, and ooh, guess what....here it came...

"I don't like the Welsh," Granddad the Great blurted suddenly as if the words had been building up inside him like a pressure cooker since he found out I was not of English blood. Here it comes, tumbleweed, rolling down the aisle towards me and gathering at my feet as if letting those around the table, not forgetting the rest of the diners in the restaurant, know that I've just been spiked with that spear of inappropriateness. I'm bloodied and dying and no one is prepared to raise a hand to help me.

Suddenly the table falls quiet, heads spin to face Granddad the Great who is now slurping the tomato soup off his spoon, and who is amazed to find the whole family wide-eyed with mouths as large as gates to castles. English castles obviously, no chance of them being good old Welsh castles now! Yep, they all turn to stare. Thank God for that because I had a feeling what he had said was going to be perfectly acceptable, but apparently not, and now they stare and they stare. All except yours truly who is as still and as frozen as an ice sculpture, waiting for someone to please, please, please just say *something*!

The silence drags on forever and I begin to melt as the awkwardness turns up the humidity. My Rosie was speechless. She hoped that her dad, my father-in-law-to-be was going to break the silence, but he wasn't. He in turn was hoping that his wife, my mother-in-law to be was not speechless, and that she'll have the ability to ask her father, my granddad-to-be to repeat, perhaps even rephrase the statement. At least that was what I was hoping was going happen. But again, nothing. Nana-in-law-to-be then all of a sudden cuts through the silence that's hung over everyone like a big soggy blanket with her peach of a statement:

"Bruce, Bruce, what did *he* say?"

"*Hey?*" My father-in-law-to-be replied, flabbergasted. All his words must have hidden from him now in their box. Either that or they had all jumped out and run away when Granddad-the-Great announced his opinion of the Welsh. By now I was not so much dying, but merely cringing, the edges of me curling up like smouldering paper. The glowing embers flushed my cheeks when...

"*Cheese*, I don't like the Welsh Cheese, what do yous (in reference to us Welsh) call it?" he questioned himself, and before he could answer I jumped in with, "Colliers?" in the hope to nip a conclusion to this episode with immediate effect. He wagged his finger at me in confirmation. He kept it wagging, and it was as if by the time he'd finished the slurp from his soup spoon, he'd magically withdrawn all the unease from the atmosphere and allowed the family to communally exhale. Maybe he wasn't the Godfather, after all, but a magic, finger-wiggling version of Dumbledore. Some family members dropped their heads in exhaustion, others' lips puckered and cheeks billowed, while I sat there with my heart clambering for an exit from my chest and my right hand affectionately squeezed by Rosie's petite left.

I looked around and my father-in-law had found his box of words once more. He pointed to my quarter-full glass of lager and asked with all the levels of authority a dad meeting his potential son-in-law should do.

"Another Carling, Carl?"

Oh Jeez! My name ain't Carl!

There had been no time for recovery from the last bout of awkwardness. The family was still heads-down and billow-cheeked when that little gem popped out.

"Dad," Rosie shouted just as she glared with horror at her mum, begging her to launch a rescue of the situation. However Rosie's mum, my mother-in-law to be, was still mortified and speechless at the inappropriate timing of her own father, my Granddad the Great to be's timing, as to when to insert a pause in his statement of Welsh cheese. An appropriate pause to grant him time enough to slurp the tomato soup off his spoon before proceeding to complete his announcement, and an inappropriate pause to leave the rest of us hanging like bodies from the gallows. She hadn't even been able to draw breath and now with her husband, my father-in-law to be, calling me by the name of one of my Rosie's exes made her choke on nothingness, struggling for air. She flapped like bird conducting a courting dance, and her mouth gobbled a mixture of sounds like the ends of words lost in her throat, and the cry of her lungs for oxygen. Bruce, Rosie's dad, my father-in-law to be, rolled his eyes with instant displeasure for his slip of the tongue and cursed his voice box for offering the wrong name from the list of boys' names at his disposal. And Carl was one name to be disposed of as of...now.

It turned out that Carl, cleaner of hotel receptions Carl, hadn't even been on the scene for ten years or more, and Bruce hadn't even met the bloke! Red with rage, Rosie removed herself from the table with as much grace as a bull in a china shop on steroids while a skilled Spaniard waved a red rag at it. I had felt exposed with just her back turned to me, but now she wasn't even beside me, and I felt naked, like a knight without his...you get what I mean. Harry, Rosie's brother; my brother-in-law to be rescued the situation. "Wanna a Grolsch, Gregory?" he spluttered. "Or how's about a Stella, Stan?" to which he received a gallant appreciative, "Yes, please," and my quarter-full glass, which suddenly looked three-quarters empty.

"Jan, Jan, what did he say?"

Nana-in-law-to-be quizzed my mother-in-law-to-be, patting her on the side of the head like a cat, having not gotten a reply from her son, Bruce, Rosie's dad and my father-in-law to be.

With hands laced together under the table, I prayed quickly for the cold November night to gust the heat of Rosie's frustration off down a handy alley, thereby returning her to her seat and my side. The conversation continued with hurdles three and four behind me. Both were rocking on their feet, but their legs stood strong and kept them upright. Hurdle five? Hmmm, where was it? How quick was it advancing? It was out there, I could feel it in the pit of my stomach, and when it loomed out of the unknown, well...I had no more time than a man suffering from premature ejaculation has to enjoy half a poke before he explodes. No sooner had Rosie returned to her seat with a windswept calm about her and mouthing an apology when it sprang upon me.

It was like jumping a junior-sized hurdle given the ease and height I cleared it with. It was the one question I had predicted, and had practiced since being invited to meet the family (in-laws to be). The reason for the rehearsed reply was there were two answers to this, both very much the truth, but both requiring the ears of a different audience. Both were the truth to the question 'What did you think when you first met our little girl?' Rehearsed reply and truth number one was...

"I first heard about my Rosie immediately after her interview. One of the interview panel members was a colleague of mine and she offered feedback to the office that

one of the ladies was certainly worthy of being offered the position. I, in turn, mirrored this comment to myself upon hearing that the successful candidate was a beautiful women, aged 24 and who was well educated having both undergraduate and post graduate degrees from Cardiff and now at Swansea University respectively. Furthermore, she demonstrated great understanding of the role applied for within Public Health. We met during Rosie's first day at work, a few weeks later, where we worked on joint programmes and pathways of care. We became friends first and foremost and love blossomed out of that." This was the family answer. This was the clean answer.

Reply and truth two varied slightly, didn't need to be rehearsed as those males reading this will shortly understand. Nevertheless, remember this is still the truth:

"My first impression of my Rosie? 'Ponytail' and 'arse'. Say these two words to any male and he'll think exactly what I thought back then, and still do to this day, and what your Mrs. hopes you aren't thinking unless it is her you're thinking of (which I bet it isn't, but worry not, your secret is safe with me). This was the lads' answer. This was the purest of truths answer. This was the truth I openly admitted to Rosie when she quizzed me, and the answer she hoped that I didn't give when her mum, my Mother-in-law to be

would no doubt enquire about.

With that, the evening seemed to settle, and I felt no longer the focal point. For a while at least. Hurdle six, seven, eight and even possibly nine? Not too sure where they were, I breezed over hurdle five with such ease that I feel I possibly cleared all future hurdles in the same leap. The wine flowed, the beer was guzzled, and before I knew it, Bruce, Rosie's dad and my father-in-law to be hand gestured for the bill by scribbling his signature in the air. (Why we still do that I don't know. When was the last time you actually signed a bill? When are we going to start miming tapping four numbers into a keypad to ask for the bill to be sent over?)

I sat back in admiration of my efforts to impress and unwrapped a mint with some swagger, I must admit. I looked around the table. Nana-in-law-to-be smiled awkwardly and then quickly shied away with the worry she might have to try to understand me, decipher the code I spoke if I struck up another conversation. The hubbub of chat quieted as I continued my journey around the table till my eyes happened upon Rosie's mum, my mother-in-law to be. Her eyes smiled adoringly between her daughter, my fiancé and wife to be, and myself. Before I could leave her to her thoughts, she leant forward, and as the question sprang into her mouth and weighed heavy within it, I suddenly saw the final hurdle of the evening bare down on me. Its height was not imposing, but knowing it was the last obstacle placed even more importance on me successfully negotiating it.

"So when did you two decide it was the real thing?" Rosie's mum, my mother-in-law to be, asked as if wanting to finish the evening on a happy note, a tale of romance, love and affection.

"Over breakfast at the MacDonald House Hotel," I blurted out with utter shock and devoid of all thought and safety net. Silence fell over the table like a two tonne heavy anvil, again.

Rosie, my wife possibly now not to be, slapped me across the arm with a simultaneous, "Hey!"

The colour of embarrassment rushed up her neck and over her face, and she did her best to hide behind her dainty cupped hands. Someone somewhere dropped their eating utensil onto their plate at what they heard and what had been more obviously implied, causing them to splatter the remains of their meal over the table. Harry, Rosie's brother and possibly not to be my brother-in-law anymore, erupted into laughter. It was him to whom I quickly looked at for some laddish approval, and got some. Even Bruce, my father-in-law (hopefully, still) approved the boastfulness of my words, as I was rapidly realising the sides of the six foot hole I'd dug myself were looking very steep. He laughed quickly and just enough so he could gain back some control over the situation as he focused on Jan, his wife, Rosie's mum and my mother-in-law to be, whose lower jaw clanged to the floor like something out of a Warner Brothers' cartoon. The corners of her mouth thankfully crept up and her mouth carefully presented a smile on her face as she realised the humour in her daughter's embarrassment.

Phew!

In my mind's eye, I swept a forearm across my brow. But oh, oh crikey...all of sudden Nana-in-law-to-be, who can't understand an honest conversation opener, but could sure start one, did so with much graveness.

"Did you feel safe in a hotel in another country on your own?" she asked innocently to Rosie. The fits of laughter in Harry's stomach caused him to double over and, at one point, gag, his eyes watering with hysterics.

"I don't think he went home to is parents' house, Mum," Rosie's mum said in an elusive tone to which she hoped her mother-in-law would catch the drift of, which she, my mother-in-law to be had, and was letting it be known with a cheeky smirk to her daughter and a nudge to her husband in the ribs, just in case he was floundering slightly. Nana-to-be turned her head back to neutral, back to face me, and I leaned forward for a reply in the hope that she could hear me.

"Um...no, Nana (to be), I didn't go home to my parents' house that night," I sheepishly said, in a bizarre whispery voice in the hope that my other family members to be wouldn't hear and Nana-to-be would! *Figure that logic out!* Then, just before Nana gave us her disbelief to how young ladies and gentleman (if that is what the males of this world today could call themselves) behave these days, Granddad the Great weighed in with a cannonball of a comment that would have blown Nana-in-law's take on today's youth not just clean out of the water, but into smithereens.

"*Lad!*" he called, already with a giggle in his throat and a smile that began to win the war of his efforts not to let show his amusement. "Lad, if she doesn't darn your socks, then chase her around the house with your dirty underpants!"

The last few words were just about recognisable as they bounded over his laughter like small ships on a choppy sea. Harry, who had picked up his drink in a lame attempt to calm his laughter and mask his big grinning lips, now backwashed his pint across the table with a burst of air and the remains of his olives. He clamped his windpipe tight as a belly full of laughter sprang up.

"Granddad!" my girlfriend (and fiancé aka wife to be) shouted and grabbed the nearest menu and brought it to her face, desperately trying to hide what was left of her crumbling dignity. I peeked around the menu as I slumped into my chair, exhaling my way into the back rest with a polite and shy laugh until my girlfriend came into view. She was sniggering merrily and was about to comment when...

"Oh dear," Bruce my father (I was still hoping)-in law to be chuckled as he rid himself of what laughter was left. He finally pulled himself together and asked with a nod, "A good night, hey?"

"Yeah" I replied. "They had to knock us up so they could turn around the room!"

The family roared into laughter and I realised that despite the potentially racist grandmother, the Welsh cheese hating grandfather, the name forgetting father and my avoidance of all manner of pitfalls that with one single line, a final riposte to the savage attacks of inappropriate spears, I ended the evening with me being the one headed for the tongue-lashing of a lifetime. And not in a good way!"

And so ends our Geezer's first memoir. We'll hear more from him later, but he already delivered to us a perfect example of where a man, even trying the hardest he possibly can, still ends up in a dark and lonely place. It makes you wonder why we even bother, doesn't it?

Number Two.

Running a close second to his penis in things that will put a man onto the express train to trouble is his excrement. A man does not have to suggest to his loved one that he would perhaps like to curl one down on her chest, while she was wrapped up in Clingfilm, for his pooh to carry him away with it down the pan. There are much simpler ways for us to get in the shit.

Like underpants that look like they've been used as a rag to clean creosote off a paint brush. Or maybe the underpants didn't do a good enough job so the brush is then plunged into the pan, smearing a thick brown, surprisingly resilient and sticky substance all over the porcelain, recently cleaned and toilet ducked by our loved one, of course. Oh, yes. That's the way to put a smile on her face.

But a way to guarantee you'll get a smile out of her is to whip out your camera and take a photo of her. *Of her.* Not of your biggest toilet deposit. She likes it when you share a lovely photo that you've taken of her looking her best. Not so much the snake like behemoth that crept its way, inch by inch out of your gaping butt hole that you insist on showing everyone. So many ways for your number two 'do-do' to get you into trouble, and yet a man can even get himself in bother over his good lady's toilet habits.

To a woman, bowel movements are done behind closed doors, if they actually take place at all. In their heads, it is better if we don't even think of them sat on the crapper, biting down and squeezing out a squelchy chocolate log. They'd rather we accepted their word that angels and fairies came while everyone was asleep and carried away their business in lavender-scented velvet bags. But as men, of course, we find their ablutions to be the funniest function they carry out, simply because they are so seemingly ashamed of the process itself. And even if the lady of the house grasps the metal and admits to taking a satisfactory number two, rather than nodding with respect and approval, the man will, of course, find a way of taking her shit and making sure that he lands himself right in it.

Jacqueline, 30, Assistant Bank Manager, Chelsea.

"Okay, so I'd been dating Warren for about eight months, and I swear we'd both simply *not go* while we were on a date. Even if we stayed at each other's apartments, if nature called we'd just leave early in the morning. You know what I mean? Okay, so we both *knew* that the other one used the bathroom, of course we did, but we didn't have to actually *do it* while the other was sat there, did we? Okay, like what if he heard? And then yeah, it got a bit more relaxed, a bit easier, and we both made sure there was always an air freshener in the bathroom so that took away a bit of the embarrassment. But it was still there. A bit of a whiff. I was really conscious about it, paranoid maybe, but he seemed to get more and more lax. Okay, so this one Tuesday morning, I'm due at the train station, going away for work, and he's offered to drive me there. I want to make sure I don't need to, umm, use the facilities at the station let alone on the train, so I *go* just before he arrives. I'm washing my hands when the doorbell goes and he's early. In a rush I don't spray, but so what? We're going straight out. Well, as he picks up my bags he lets out this vile noise from his backside and he pulls a face like he's in a Carry On movie, doesn't even excuse himself or apologise. He actually looks a little proud of himself so in a moment of pique I decide to beat him at his own game. "You think that's bad?" I ask him and point at the closed bathroom door. "You should go in there and smell what I did!"

I thought I'd put him in his place but you know what he does? He puts my bags down. That's what he does. He puts my bags down and he goes and smells what I did in there. Actually inhaling deeply through his nostrils, like he's at a wine tasting. He turns around and nods at me, glowing. "Good work," and although I'm chilled to my very core I manage to think 'I've done my ladette bit and that's that.' Yeah, that's that? Until it becomes his stock story on every night out from then on. My friends, his friends, new friends, work mates, family. "You should go in there and smell what I did," becomes my fucking catchphrase. Can you imagine that? Idiot."

So while women curl one down with more

guile than James Bond, for men, the mantra is the bigger the better, and if we can induce our own hysterics with a cacophony of raspberries to accompany our crap then we've really hit the back of the net. Of course, if someone else hears it too, then it's like we've won the Champions League Final and an Olympic Gold all in one go.

You see, as with all of his achievements, whether it be on the field of sport, work or Call of Duty Black Ops, man simply has to show off what they've done. Size, girth, length, pain inflicted. These are all key indicators for the male to determine and define his own masculinity, and I'm not talking about his endowment policy. "Massive" is not a word a woman wants to hear when her mate returns from the bathroom. "Lost half a stone there, love," equally does not go down too well. Essentially if a man wants to get himself in the shit, well it's obvious what he needs to talk about publicly. Of course there are limits, even for men. You don't want to be announcing that you've, "Just dropped the kids off at the pool," the first time you meet the potential future mother-in-law, but the problem with men is that such discipline is hard to maintain, and we're far to open to people peering behind our curtain to see our inner workings. Literally.

If a man gets away with it in those early months and his good lady is able to turn a blind eye, and of course nose, away from his toiletry tribulations then things between them have every chance of blossoming into the triumphant romance filled with passion and respect. He is working hard at being a good boyfriend and his efforts, which become less and less of a chore with every passing day without a telling off, are making her feel like a million dollars. He believes he can do nothing wrong and then they have 'The Conversation.' Where are we going? What do we mean to each other? Do you see us together in ten years time? Despite being sure he is going to kneecap himself halfway through, he makes it and they decide to move in together. Now this is where things can really hit the skids.

One of the most naturally occurring developments that takes place when a couple move in together for the first time is that their two piles of dirty clothes become one. Pretty knickers and sweaty rugby shirts become a living, breathing symbiotic entity held together by the magic of static. The washing becomes not a job but a 'shared activity,' something they do together. One loads the machine, the other hangs up the wet clothes. Poetry in motion. But, of course, a man will find a way to destroy this bastion of bliss. He will find a way to let his dirty clothes lead him down a very dark path. Amanda found this out to her disgust when her boyfriend, Paul, left her a lovely surprise in the wash basket.

Amanda, 33, Gym Instructor, Devon.

"Now don't get me wrong, I've never had a problem being the one who does the washing. It isn't an issue. To be fair, he is actually better at ironing than me, and he's happy for me to throw a few of my things on his ironing pile if he's doing work shirts. But this one day, I'm sorting the whites from the colours, I'm sorting the delicates, you know the score? And he's got this pair of white, well y-fronts I guess, that he wears to the gym, and they're a bit grim but he says they're comfortable under his shorts, and I pick them up and I swear to God I think that maybe one of my socks has got stuck inside and I open them up..."

She pauses, raises her hand up to her mouth.

"It was like he'd painted Marmite in there. A three-inch-long streak of Marmite.

Trust me, when it's in his pants, there's no choice between love it or hate it. I let out this almighty yell and threw them away from me. They sat there, in the corner of the kitchen until he got home from work. I'll tell you, he does the washing these days."

The main problem with the skid-marked pair of underpants is man's inability to learn from them. Once is enough as far as the ladies are concerned. From then on there should be a strict regime of checking and where possible double checking that any such branded boxers or briefs make it to the wash basket. Most women would recommend regular tactical wiping in between actual bowel movements as a precautionary measure. There is, however, hope for man that this route towards Big Trouble Boulevard is not as downhill as it first appears. Some women will simply put up with it. Could it be that it is easier to ignore such a thing than to actually make it a big steaming issue? Maybe it is just that they can find the superhuman resolve required for a woman to overcome her fear of the skid-mark, or it could just be a generational thing as our old friend Gloria demonstrates.

Gloria, 68, Retired, Swansea.

"See, I've got so used to it now that I just boils them, like. He's been the same for years. I don't know if he doesn't wipe proper, like, or if he follows through but it's not worth falling out over, like, is it? So I've got a big pot, don't use it for anything else, mind you, and I boils them up. Some of his older pants now, they've got a permanent stain, but no one else sees them except me and him. And it's pointless getting him new ones. He's set in his ways, like, see."

Even if all women found the acceptance of a Gloria and all men become as vigilant in the skid-mark monitoring as our partners would want us to be, if stained underpants became a thing of the past, there is still another 'mark' that will count against us men. One that impinges upon the porcelain of our very souls. Or at least you would think it does, the fuss that women make over it. I am of course talking about the shitty staining of the toilet bowl.

Carl, 23, Post-Graduate Student, Manchester.

"Right, I think it's important to highlight in the first instance that waiting around until after the flush has finished to see whether I've left some permanent marker of my toilet activity is simply not in my nature. Come on? Is it in anybody's nature? No, it's not. Especially not men. Gone are the days when the newspaper was carried proudly under the arm on the way to the loo, indicating that the throne was going to be occupied for quite some time. Life has changed. No one has the time to commit to that sort of luxury anymore. It's a case of get in there, get the job done and get out. Look, it could be that this behaviour is to blame for many of the world's health problems, like prostate issues, you know, but we're always *doing* something. Standing around to check that what we've already done has properly gone away just is not an agenda item. Anyway, all it takes is another flush and whatever's there is gone, right? So I don't see what all the fuss is about."

Carl's housemate, Emma, respectfully disagrees. She is quick to highlight that both Carl and their third housemate, Pascal, a Master's student originally from Lens in France, have more than enough spare time to occasionally ensure a clean loo, citing the amount of computer games and drinking sessions the two enjoy. Emma feels that it shows a deep-rooted lack of self respect in addition to them not caring about how their actions impinge upon her.

Emma, 22, Post-Graduate Student, Manchester.

"You really want to hear about this, do you? And you think it'll help? Make men consider their behaviour? It won't! That I do know. But if you want to hear it, then here goes. First of all, even animals do not leave their filth just lying there. Cats, from a very young age, will bury their business. Do horses empty their bowels and then turn around and examine their deposits? No! So why should I have to look at the left-behinds that those two idiots have not got the good grace to clean up. I've seen it all. An unflushed pan with a monster turd wearing soiled toilet paper like a little hat? Check! Pebble dashing after a night on the beer with a curry chaser? Check! An over cooked chicken nugget just floating there, challenging me to make it go away? Check! The classic brown streak? Goes without saying, but, yes, check! And my favourite? A brown...something on the back of the actual toilet seat. Seriously! How did it get there? It's physically impossible but all the same, it was right there, winking at me. A piece of shit on the toilet seat? Check! So I try talking to them and nothing changes except the level of school boy sniggering. So I buy some bleach, rubber gloves and a toilet brush. If they used it just once, I'd die happy."

Carl and Emma's flatmate, Pascal, remains unimpressed. His French accent adds a certain something to his sentiment.

Pascal, 26, Post-Graduate Student, Manchester.

"She wants me to clean my shit with that little brush? I tell her to go fuck herself!"

Not all women will be as unforgiving as an Emma and hopefully not all men are as selfish as a Pascal and, while the bathroom will never be a place where a couple sits and hold hands while one of them drops a load, harmony can be achieved. However, even if the man works on his sphincter becoming more accurate than the gun barrel at the start of a

Bond movie *and* learns how to use the toilet brush, it is still his inherent obsession with what comes out of his backside that will get him dumped. Richard and Jenny moved in together after two years of dating and had gone another two years without a major bust up. That was until one fateful night when Richard needed to go to the toilet and this is where Jenny starts this particular tale.

Jenny, 27, Dietician, Dublin.

"We're watching television and Richard gets up, gives me a little smile and leaves the room. No fuss. No jokes. He just doesn't do that, doesn't see the point in it, I guess. You know what? I genuinely thought he was that one bloke out there who *had* gone beyond that childish, pointless toilet humour. I'm sat there, not even feeling the need to think about what he's doing in the loo...when he starts laughing!"

She gives Richard a glare. He shoves virtually his whole fist into his mouth to stop his laughter. His eyes glow red and tears run down his cheeks. Jenny shakes her head.

"And that's the noise I hear coming from the toilet. He's in there laughing himself to death. And that's not the worst of it! Next thing, the door opens, I hear him shuffle out, still laughing like a moron, and then he shuffles back and the door closes again and it is only then that I realise that I've not heard the toilet being flushed!"

This proves to be too much for Richard and he virtually explodes into hysterics. Jenny crosses her legs and rests one elbow on her knee, her hand supporting her head as she purposely does not look at him. The room should, of course, be thick with tension. Richard should have realised by now that he has, for the umpteenth time, crossed a far from imaginary line. It would appear that such a line is beyond the imagination of a mere man. After some minutes, Richard pulls himself together.

Richard, 31, Tennis Coach, Dublin.

"I'll be honest with you, she's right. I wasn't one to fart or to make crass bodily function jokes, it really was not my style. What goes on in there is between a man and himself, simple as, but that time I realised something special was happening, that what I was creating was simply *not normal*. I sat down, got myself settled, as settled as you can, and started *going*. I was about halfway through, or so I thought, when I thought to myself, *hey, this is big*, and it wasn't in a celebratory, backslapping kind of way. It was just in a *something different* kind of way. But it kept coming, and I'm starting to think, like, is this where the Cloverfield monster came from? And I get the giggles and then as I finish I take a peek down in between my legs and I swear to God I thought that thing was going to bite me. There was six inches of it out of the water, let alone what was below. And I knew then that I simply *had* to take a photo. *A tissue free photo*. So I ran out and got my phone, took a picture and then did the necessary."

Richard bursts out laughing again. He starts to pull his mobile phone from his back pocket.

"Do you want to see?"
Jenny gives Richard a look that stops him in his tracks. The phone slips from sight but Richard's grin does not.

Jenny, 27, Dietician, Dublin.

"Enough people have seen *that* already! Do you realise who has had to endure seeing that? Me for one! Dozens of times. He'll make out he's showing me something different and there it is, like Mister Whippy has started doing chocolate flavoured ice cream! And all of our friends of course. He seems to think that everyone wants to see it, that everyone will wet their pants at the very sight of his mess! Christmas last year, he goes and gets drunk and shows my dad! Can you imagine that? I was watching them chatting and it looked all intense and for a fleeting moment I actually thought he was asking my dad, you know, for my hand in marriage, and then my dad cringes away from him and I see he's got his phone in his hand, and I just know which picture he's got on the screen. The thing is, it's not like he's the only one, is it? They're all the same. What I want to know is if they all have to dash out to get their phones or if there's more planning. Like, do they actually take their phones in just in case it's worth taking a picture of?"

Richard, it would seem, is a master at getting himself in trouble. Whereas most men would have kept their mouths shut and let their partner's rant run out of steam, he instead stokes the fire.

Richard, 31, Tennis Coach, Dublin.

"Well I do now! I doubt I'll ever create anything like that again, but you never know, do you? But I'll tell you what, Jenny's right. I know a good few blokes who have taken a poo picture. There was this one afternoon when I'd invited a few mates over to watch the match and we had new neighbours moving in next door, so I ask them over for a drink and they end up staying for the second half. So there's me, Jenny, my three mates, the new couple next door and his brother, and one of the players makes a mistake and someone says 'that's shit' and my immediate response is, 'that's not shit, this is shit' and I pull out my phone and flash the picture around. Well next thing you know, all the lads have got their phones out and we're passing them around comparing poo sizes. The women were just sat there, mouths open, shaking their heads. Look, it's just a bit of fun. It's not worth getting annoyed over. But I will tell you one thing. Mine was definitely the biggest!"

Jenny can take no more at this point, which is pretty much the sentiment of most women when it comes to their man's close encounters of the turd kind. Strangely, on the whole (or is that 'on the hole'?), men are extremely aware that talking about, sharing or showing their excrement is not normal. However, it truly seems that given the right stimulus, they are helpless but to respond like a monkey throwing faeces at the zoo. If this type of behaviour continues, it is very apparent that as far as our number one sweetheart goes, we are always going to be number two.

Memoir of a Geezer

Our Geezer, (or, as you may have started to think of him already, our anti-Geezer, super un-cool) just like any man, has a faecal fable to relate to us. However, so powerful are our hero's powers and abilities to get it catastrophically wrong, that with one error of judgement he is able to alienate not one woman but three in one go. It is a tale that he hopes will not leave you, unlike him, down in the dumps.

Rhian, Nana and the Bracken Bush

"Dear old Nana was the grandparent that, as kids, you visited perhaps twice a year, always at Christmas and then that other random, out of the blue, "We're going to Nana's in hour, so go wash and clean yourself up," time. Obviously the latter horrifyingly falls on you with as much terror and surprise as the empty shell of a dead spider from the loft rafters. But there's nothing you can do to change the fact you are going, simple as that.

The visit to Nana's is long, as is the wait to stop

behaving beyond your years. My brother David and I could remember those few months back to our last visit, at Christmas 1989 and knew that the journey did at least have some pay off. Another of Nana's grandsons lived with her occasionally and was serving his country somewhere in Europe, and the time it took for us to be let off the leash, we'd head straight for his room to find his sweets, and more importantly his pornography magazines. Success was just a matter of moments away (as long as we hadn't been rumbled and he hadn't moved them). But first, we sat, accepted the ruffling of Nana's hand through our hair, the whitened, creepy cobweb-like haired lips shrivelling up like an anus to kiss our cheeks. We smiled falsely to acknowledge the, "My, haven't you grown," statements and to hide our dissatisfaction of being offered only rich tea biscuits with our powdered milk tea, lumps of which still rotated in the swirl of the stir within the cup like planets following their orbit. *The leash, the leash shall be loosened* I thought, and then there would be boobs.

However in 1990, the second biannual visit to Nana's house never came, instead she was coming to us.

Permanently.

When I first heard this, my initial concern was

that David and I would have to share a room again. That threw a spanner in the works in that it would disrupt how I liked to spend my 'alone time'. How I sighed with relief when I learnt she was to be dumped in the local old peoples' home! She had become frail and dependable on others, and though the family rallied, a fall here and a scare there led the heads of the families to acknowledge that their efforts were not enough. That summer Nana sold up and moved into the residential home down the road from us. Okay, so I feel guilty for thinking this way now that I am an adult, but I remember hailing this as a triumph back then. Did it occur to me that now she was just a mile and half down the round that I would have to visit her more often? I can't say with any certainty. Nevertheless, it was Nana's moving-in day and, with our parents fulfilling their offer to help, my brother and I called on the kids of the street for some fun.

Rhian came out, and we were glad. Her boyfriend at the time, Richard, also came out, which we weren't so glad about. Rhian was seventeen, as were Richard and I. My brother was two years younger. Rhian was regarded as the cleverest girl at school and was therefore classed as a bit of a 'Plain Jane Superbrain', but I had noticed over the last year or so how she had developed. She had developed a fun sense of humour. She had developed her own style of dressing. She had developed very pert little boobies. It also appeared that she was developing an appetite for sexual expression, and I slowly came to realise that I wanted to share in this with her. I knew for sure I would be better for her to experiment with than her current idiot in tow.

Two weeks ago, Rhian had invited Richard into her house whilst she was home alone. Richard's surname was Mong, and although as an adult it is not a term I approve of the use of, at the time I believed that if anyone lived up to their name, Richard certainly did. He had declined Rhian's offer. It was bad enough that he'd knocked her back, but what did he expect to gain by telling us? Sympathy? After what seemed like hours of coaxing, Richard agreed to let Rhian dance for him. Naked. The condition was that only he could watch from the street...(*of course!*).

Rhian lived in a townhouse on the lower side of the street. As the street was built into a mountainside, the second floor of the house, where her bedroom was located, was at street level, so Richard need not go anywhere, but take a seat on the front wall and enjoy the view. What Rhian hadn't stipulated was that the rest of us, that being my brother, our friend Gareth and I couldn't watch from...say Gareth's bedroom? Gareth's bedroom was on the third floor of his parents' house just one house down on the opposite side of the road to Rhian's. It offered us a perfect view of the front windows of Rhian's house. We knew we had a few minutes (Rhian had told Richard so), yet nevertheless, the three of us jammed ourselves all the way up both narrow flights of steps in as much of a frenzy as a pack of wilder-beast clearing the river banks of hungry crocs.

With three pairs of beady eyes peering wide-eyed over the window ledge, we ogled as Rhian drew back her curtains and stood on her bed...naked. She danced to music we couldn't hear, her mouth formed words we couldn't make out, and she swayed. To this very day I can see her. Oh, yeah. I'm seeing her right now. But, damn it, I can also see Richard, stiff as a statue (I make no apologies for the pun). He sits on the wall for a while and then he climbs down from the wall and walks down the street, through his garden gate and disappears. By this time, we'd all tracked Richard the Mong down the road, wondering *what the heck* he was doing, where he was going, and more importantly, why he was not watching Rhian dancing for him. To track him, we had to peer forward over the window sill. Rhian, obviously wondering what he was doing, had also leaned forward and pressed her body against the glass window. Suddenly both we and Rhian realised our error. Firstly, we weren't watching the nakedness of Rhian swaying seductively, but watching a boy saunter off down the street. Secondly, we had peered too far over the window sill to track Richard just as Rhian had leaned against the window to do the same, her boobs pressed flat against the glass. Suddenly, in horror the collective 'we' had spotted each other. Rhian had spotted us, we ducked and Rhian scrambled for her bedroom curtains.

Anyhow, I digress. The point is that after two weeks, Rhian had come out to hang out with us, and I guess it was a sign of her 'growing' as a person that she held no resentment towards us for enjoying her dancing skills. No matter what the reason it seemed she was over any embarrassment she may have felt, and for this I was glad. Glad because perhaps she'd be frustrated with Richard's lack of enthusiasm for her body and how seductively it could move. Maybe, just maybe she'd be keen to flaunt herself in front of one of us who obviously took the advantage to peep at the peep show and would love to do so again. And maybe a bit more.

So, in my head, I had the stirrings of a plan to steal Rhian from Richard. My brother, Rhian, (unfortunately) Richard Mong and I, along with some other street rabble, headed towards the mountains above the street and its adjoining estate, at the end of which sat Nana's new home. The bracken was a lush green and its leaves new and vibrant. Perfect for weaving your way through and losing your opponent in many of the games played that summer's day. Let's be honest, it was a more innocent time back then. Playing was simply that. It all came from the imagination, not from a computer chip. We were active, we ran, we had fun. We'd occasionally nick a few cans from someone's house and get a little bit drunk but that wasn't all the time. Life was just about having fun!

As the afternoon moseyed along, so we did across the mountain, and so did (albeit, unexpectedly so) a pooh in my bowel. Game by game we trekked until the mountain veered steeply down to the abandoned railway line. The bracken thinned here and my hopes of nestling down next to Rhian beneath the fern leaves, which I had managed to strategically do all afternoon, vanished quickly like the sun over the mountains in the distance. From about midday I had noticed frequent but tiny puffs of a putrid stench emanating from my bottom, which grew heavier throughout the day. By around 2pm, my bum cheeks began to ache a little and sitting down felt like squishing the mucky contents of my bowel across the walls of my intestines. By 4pm, I had deliberately hidden behind the old oak tree during a game of 'kick-the-can' as to fight my body's natural (and by now eager) urge to rid itself of its waste. There I stood, legs together, fully extended while trying to tighten my sphincter as the peristaltic movements became stronger. Suddenly my right hand was required to clench the cheeks of my arse, to pull them tighter together, in an attempt to stop my bowels from simply flushing themselves out.

I was terrified of shitting myself. Rhian would simply not be impressed. The pressures of my rolling anal contractions were now immense. Powerful enough for me to think my thumb (which was currently busy clenching my arse cheeks together) could and should be used as a butt plug. Why, you may ask, was I putting myself through this? Why would I not dash home, when it was all of a ten-minute walk, four minute run? Well, the answer is twofold. The first was I had spent all day stretching Rhian's and my friendship, stretching it so that it stepped into the realm of attraction and curiosity, and

I wanted to see how far I could get before we headed home. I wanted my just-desserts and have Rhian dance on me under the dense bracken of the mountain. The second was it was all too late. The point of no return was around 2pm when my bowels sank into the cheeks of my arse and ached in discomfort under the strain of its heavy load. A dash home would only cause my arse to explode like pent up water released from a blocked hose.

We were playing hide-and-seek (like I said, it was a simpler time) and I had hidden behind a monstrous nettle bush just below the dirt track that cut across the mountain and above the wooden fence and sty that open onto the reception gardens of Nana's new nursing home. I blinked with surprise at that moment when I saw dear old Nana being taken for a walk by my mum and Auntie Jules. Behind them on the drive way, Dad and Uncle Terry were unloading the last pieces of furniture from the van: a reclining armchair and her stuffed cat, Oodles. By the time I was found (a good 15 minutes later), Nana was settling into her new apartment and Mum, Dad and other members of the family were finding homes for all her ornaments, for Oodles and decorating walls with paintings of babbling waters under arches of stone bridges and so on. Dusk was falling and we (the rabble from the street) decided it was time for a game of spin the bottle. Okay, *I* thought it was time for a game of spin the bottle!

We gathered in circle and my brother placed the discarded wine bottle he'd found during 'kick-the-can' in the middle. It was agreed that those the bottle chose, would leave the circle and go around the back of the disused outbuilding for privacy. Time ticked by and kisses were exchanged. Richard Mong would only play when he could kiss Rhian. Rhian seemed happy to kiss whoever was selected. This I was glad about. Jimmy seemed to get overexcited when the bottle pointed towards any of the boys and looked disappointed when he (obviously) had to spin the bottle again. Finally, as we were all getting anxious to get home as curfews loomed large in our minds, Rhian and I walked around the back of the outbuilding. Richard sulked. I had watched enough Channel 4 late night films and episodes to some TV series to know how to kiss. Oh yeah, I knew how to lay on an impressionable kiss, and I knew how, in the movies or late night TV episodes, such a kiss nearly always led to nakedness. I stepped in whilst clearing my throat and she smirked and wet her lips when something moist popped across the inside of my pants. *Across the back of my pants!*

It had been hours since my body first tried to rid itself of a stool and had come up against resistance. I hadn't resorted to using my DIY butt plug, and now it was suddenly too late. Something had pushed my body too far. Perhaps it was overexcitement at the prospect of kissing the not-so-private dancer. Perhaps bowels have a weight restriction which once exceeded cause the contents to be forcefully removed. Because this *was* forceful, my shit was on its way, hurtling down my inners with no way back, just like a ski jumper. My arse muscles clenched, the ring hole screwed up and my right hand slid in between my butt cheeks. My eyes bulged, watered in fact, and I swear I made some high pitched squeal like a guinea pig. In a panic I spotted a bank of raspberry bushes, through which not much could be seen. They backed onto the steep verge of the mountain down to the old railway track. I would like to think I would have apologised to Rhian as I ambled like Jake-the-peg with a wooden leg up my arse over to the raspberry bushes. I would like to think I had, but by now I had the sweats and I swear my pores were now puffing guffs of pooh in an attempt to shed my body of its brown matter in any way possible.

Within meters of the fruit bush, both my belt and jeans had been undone and they fell to the ground. The back of my pants were splattered with bits and pieces, covered with a paste like the smearing of a drying out bottle of Tippex on a page, just with a heavy hint of brown.

"Paper," I shouted to the group in a squeal of horror as my bowels felt like they were rattling, turd frenzied and clanging against the inside of my cavity in a desperate panic.

"He's shitting himself, he's *shitting himself*," Rhian roared in hysterics as she just about managed to run from behind the outbuilding with laughter making her legs as wobbly as jelly. The group shot up like a bunch of Meer cats detecting a threat with disbelief and a strange desire to see for themselves, a type of curiosity written across their grins. They all made a sudden burst for the raspberry bush.

Abruptly, (I can only describe it as I felt it), my bowels imploded. They seemed to crunch together into a ball of worms, leaving a feeling of nothing, a void inside the lower cavity of my trunk. Next, every nerve raced the same signal from my knotted bowels, up my spine to register in my mind, the signal displayed in the form of words that read: '*Squat, and squat NOW*' in big neon lights that blinked like the illuminations of fun-fair. Instinct spread my feet as far as the waist line of my jeans and pants would let them, and I dipped into a squat position, just as the rabble from our street, including Rhian and my brother, sprinted around the sides of the raspberry bush. My face grew thin and haunted and my bowel now began to spasm, sending all it had down to the hole in my arse. It opened as quick as a blink of an eye and left me with a groan that did not draw to a harrowing close until the remaining slop that chundered out of my arse had fallen into a gloppy pile on the floor, topping the initial hard stools like syrup topping over a chocolate brownie.

THUD! THUD! THUD!

To my left, my brother was consumed with hilarity, so much so he'd forgotten to breathe between laughs and was purple in the face with giggles. When he did remember to breathe, his arms pointed and flapped around like a puppet whose master was having a heart attack.

THUD! THUD! THUD!

The sound came again and I registered that there had been an initial three thuds just moments before, but events in the immediacy had taken a higher priority in the here and now. To my right, Gareth was virtually choking on his own tongue. He was doubled over and retching from as deep as his toes. Nothing but the lining of his stomach came up, but I noticed he had closed his nostrils. I hadn't registered the stench that I had deposited on the earth, shit was still dripping out of me now like a Slush Puppy from the end of a straw and I was just concentrating on not getting it on my jeans. I took a second to glance down and realised that despite me efforts my underpants at least were already destined for the bin. Gareth turned away and with distance and closed off nostrils between him and the smoking mound of poop on the floor, he broke into an uncontrollable body bouncing giggle.

THUD! THUD! THUD!

The noise rang out for a third time and my ears picked up the direction to which the sound came from: behind me. But its registration stopped there as running away from me was Rhian, and the hope of ever seeing her dance for me up close and personal ran with her, only faster. Could I dream of witnessing any future nakedness? I fear the answer was a distinctive no. And I don't blame her. If I had seen pooh coming out of my potential suitor's bare and bulging sphincter like a high pressured Mr Whippy ice cream machine, then I too would have had reservations.

THUD! THUD! THUD!

"Oh crap! Look around... No! Don't look

around," Gareth blurted out amongst a laugh that was as hard as my thighs were under the strain to stop me from falling into my own pile of shit. My brother tracked Gareth's line of sight from the opposite side of the raspberry bush, up over a tall dark stained fence, over a ground floor building containing a series of high back reclining chairs angled towards a large TV mounted on the far wall, and up to a large floor-length window on the first floor apartment, where three pairs of eyes looked out, not at Gareth, but at the naked, excrement smeared buttocks of...

THUD! THUD! THUD!

The 'bells' of my doom echoed out for the final time as this set of wallops (which was now clearly glass thundering in its frame) achieved its purpose, to grab the attention of the bear who was shitting in the woods...me. Still in squat position, with my arse still sticking out and my sphincter looking like the mouth of a baby who had eaten chocolate and then tried to deny it, I spun my head around and looked over my right shoulder in the direction of where the THUD! THUD! THUD! came from. In mid-head turn, confusion buzzing in my mind: *'Glass? A window? On a Mountain?'* I questioned. Within the millisecond it took for my line of sight to meet that of my brother's and Gareth's, my confusion had cleared away like a light mist in a gale force wind.

"Oh shit," I said.

Staring out at me were the eyes of Nana and my parents, who had been showing her the wonderful view from her new apartment as part of the settling in process. It was, and still is for that matter, a horrific family portrait that belongs in some haunted house. Nana sat back erect in her high back chair, her forearms resting along the length of the chair's armrests and her hands hung limply off the edge, still except for the creepy tapping of her fingertips against the fabric-bare weave. Her eyes were ablaze with disgust and shock. To her right my mum stood rooted to the spot and gray with denial.

It was as if my sphincter had the curse of Medusa's eyes.

My father was only there for a few moments, just enough to catch him in the frame of this ghastly picture, but with an element of blur to him as if he was already in motion, and one of haste too. He was stood beside Nana's chair, his teeth gritted against each other until his tongue rolled over and its belly protruded through the gaps between his upper and lower teeth. His eyes were bulging and I thought they just might pop out of their sockets and wobble on their stalks.

"*Paper*," I screamed at Gareth and my brother. "Get me some fucking toilet paper." Two things quickly became evident to me in less than a moment takes to become a moment. One was that there was no toilet paper available to one who shits in the woods and, two, Dad was now out of the haunted family portrait and moving with haste...straight for me. I know this as I could see him hurtling down the steps through the glass encased stairwell.

"*Ferns!*" I screamed higher and more frantically. "*Ferns!* Get me some fucking ferns!" Dave, my brother had also witnessed my dad's efforts and it dampened his flaming laugh instantly like a fire blanket smothering a lit chip-pan. He spun around frantically looking for a bracken bush like a dog chasing its tail. Round and around he went. . .

"Fucking ferns!" I shrieked like a baby who's lost its dummy, and that shot my brother off in the direction of a bracken bush just meters away, where he furiously pulled the stems of ferns from out of the ground, returning with two handfuls, stalks at the bottom and fern leaves at the top, *splayed out to maximise coverage.* I thought, 'Skill,' as there was a lot of wiping over a large surface area to be done.

Having quickly checked for bugs and creepy

crawlies, I placed my hand on the back of the fern leaves for leverage and swiped through the valley of my arse. I spun the leafy pad over and swiped again. Gareth had now returned with additional leafy paper substitutes and I wiped with fury. I had made my fifth swipe and inspected it in the failing light of the day to judge just how many more were needed, when my brother let of a muddled yell of shock and humour. I spun to my right to see that Dad had just made it over the fence's sty, with the outhouse the next landmark from where I was just seconds away from being at arms' length.

"Arh, *DAD!*" I yelled, followed by a series of school girl screams. "Ferns, I need more pissing ferns." By now I was jumping up and down on the spot like a lamb learning to leap and suddenly this felt comfortable. Why did it feel comfortable? Because my frigging bladder was just about to explode as if hit by one of those bouncing bombs in the Dam-busters war films.

"Arh, *DAD!*" I yelped. "Arh piss!"

"*I'm pissing myself!*" It suddenly occurred to me. Not so much occurred as slapped me in the face. The time it had taken for me to realise that I needed to piss, and to glance over to my dad, (who was launching himself over the uneven mountainous terrain like a fucking bouncing bomb) was too long. My bladder has crumbled against the weight of my urine which stank like sugar puffs and was pouring into my shit smeared pants. And now my furious father was just a few arm lengths away. I was in all sorts of trouble!

"Arh piss, ferns, *Dad...Arh!*"

I yelled and took flight, quite literally, over the raspberry bush. I had fallen over my jeans and pants, which were still draped over my ankles. My brother roared with laughter, enough to split his sides, I reckon, especially so when I scrambled onto my feet and stumbled through the bush with one hand extended out for counter-balance and the other grasping my penis and ball sack, whilst I screeched like a baby pig being taken away from its mother. Once on the other side of the raspberry bush, with a mere few hundred scratches on my legs, I attempted to run up the mountainside, my dad in pursuit and my jeans and pants still clinging to my ankles. My brother describes it, looking back, as a manic x-rated Benny Hill comedy moment as our dad and I are running round mole hills, trees, bushes, through bracken as if being fast forwarded. All that was missing was the high tempo music. Twice I managed to dodge my father's grasp. On both occasions I had squirmed free. Twice I spun around, nearly pissing all over his shins and stopping dad dead in his tracks, whilst I continued to peg it across the mountain.

At one point I ran with both hands in the air like I just didn't care, some semi-starkers 90's raver but with my penis wobbling about like a hose attached to a gushing tap in front of me. However, having foiled two attempts, the pursuit was short-lived, and soon enough, my dad wrestled me to the floor and was pulling up my pants, grunting. Words obviously failed him at this point. After all, it's not every day you open your mother's (my grandmother's) curtains to see your eldest son taking a shit. But you have to admit, of all the apartments, of all the possible sights she could see, Nana didn't just have the room with a view, she had the room with the pooh!

I was bundled into the back of the car with my mucky pants smearing my arse cheeks at the rear and damping my pubes with sugar puff cereal smell to the front. This was not before a towel borrowed from the old people's home was used to cover the back seat. Mum was already waiting in the passenger's seat with the engine idling. Within minutes of reaching home I was pushed by the scruff of my neck into the bathroom, where this seventeen-year-old boy had his arse scrubbed vigorously by his mummy. Unfortunately this fact was shared around the neighbourhood by my thoughtful and considerate brother. I'll not go into the names I used to be called but enough to say that I still cannot face chocolate ice cream.

Nothing ever came of my relationship with Rhian. Of course it didn't. She'd watched me curl one down in front of my family. What more could we possibly have to share?"

At least our Geezer, even from this relatively young age, was able to recognise the error of his ways and acknowledge that public displays of defecation are frowned upon. It's just a shame that he learnt little from the lesson to take forward in life...

Driving Miss Crazy.

Of course, it's not just our body parts or our bodily functions with which man will get it wrong. Oh, no. There are a whole host of accessories ready, willing and able to take an active part in our downfall. Funnily enough though, it is the one most often referred to as a penis extension that takes centre stage right now, and there, gleaming like the most important thing in a man's life, it is: the motor car. Now you're probably thinking, 'Come on, just how many ways can a car help a man screw things up?' My advice to you is remove your socks now, because you are going to need every digit you can find, and counting with your penis is not to be encouraged.

Generally, it seems that it is something men grow out of when they are in their thirties and then migrate back towards afterwards, but certainly for the younger stud and for gentlemen of a certain age, a polished and shiny car is a status symbol. Maybe it is their way of reflecting that they care about their own looks and appearance. Maybe it's their way of showing that they are meticulous and have an eye for detail. Or maybe, just maybe, it's their unknowing way of showing that they're either too young to realise that they should be spending that kind of effort on their lady, or worse, that they're now too old to remember.

Stacey, 19, Beautician, Cheltenham.

"The thing is like, right, I gets that he loves his car, and that, but all he seems to do is clean the thing. It's not like he drives it anywhere. He spends a fortune on waxes and polishes and cloths, and that, but if I ask him to take me out for a drive in it, he's always whining about the cost of petrol or putting unnecessary miles on the clock, whatever that means. He spends more time with that thing than he does with me, and I'll tell you what, if he spent as long stroking and rubbing me as he does that car of his, then I'd save a bloody fortune in batteries! Maybe then I'd be able to give him some money for petrol and he could actually drive the damn thing!"

The younger generation are not the only ones making this type of mistake.

Liz, 58, Drama Teacher, Windsor.

"Elliot would disappear for hours at a time. Truly hours. It took me a while to realise, of course, because one doesn't necessarily stand at the door and wave off one's husband as he takes the Jag out for a drive. But one day he said he was 'going out to the car' and I thought nothing more of it until I started to make dinner. I went out to the garage to get some vegetables and there he is, sat in the driver's seat, polishing the dash, listening to Radio Bloody Four. He hasn't heard me so I creep up to the window and give the glass a little rap. Silly bugger nearly had a heart attack. Tries to explain it as his 'alone time'. I didn't realise how hurtful such sentiments could be until I heard them directed at me! Gosh, to think he'd rather clean his car than spend time with me. I almost wish there'd been another woman. He's not so keen on making sure his Ford Focus is nice and shiny, that's for certain!"

There is one fact that every man across the globe believes to be true, that they are the greatest driver on the planet, and that it is only a serious of unfortunate events that have prevented them from becoming the Formula One World Champion. Now this in itself is not a flaw that is going to see them dumped or kipping in the spare room: everyone harbours dreams and aspirations. It's a healthy aspect of normal life that we should all want more for ourselves and that we should all push ourselves forward in our quest to achieve our maximum potential. However, when a man chooses to verbally express his Jedi-enhanced driving skills to his mates in the pub while his clearly bored girlfriend stands there, bottle of Blue WKD in hand, staring at her white stilettos, then if nothing else he should realise he is going to be the one buying the kebabs on the way home, and that the likelihood of a sexual encounter taking place is diminishing with every hairpin bend he's apparently taken since leaving the M25.

Unknown male, old enough to know better, Chav, Croydon.

"So I cuts from the outside lane, right across the front of this Porsche that's got to be doing, like, ninety, and I just leave him, like, like he's fucking standing there, and I comes off the fucking motorway and, you know, at that junction, yeah, there's that double apex, well I'm in third and I'm touching seventy all the way around it, mate, fucking back end is fucking right on the edge of losing it, yeah, but I've got it under control and then it straightens out and I'm hammering down past that pub, you know, that pub, what's it called, The Lamb, that's it innit, yeah, and you can see everyone in the beer garden fucking turning to have a look, cos let's face it, my fucking Renault is the dog's fucking bollocks, dump valve fucking pumping, music pumping out the speakers, mate, fucking hell, you should have seen me, like fucking Schumacher, I'm telling you. If the insurance hadn't fucked me over I'd be fucking racing by now, and the fucking copper I went past, he didn't even bother, mate, didn't even bother cos he knew there'd be no catching me."

Somehow, seemingly without taking a pause for breath let alone a drink, he's finished his pint. He hands the empty glass to the comatose girlfriend and utters a sentence that would make any woman that overheard it realise that maybe their fella wasn't quite so bad after all.

"Be a good girl, love, run along to the bar, will ya?"

While not all men are as so delusional as our friend here, there is still a risk that the arrogance that goes with being even the meekest of greatest drivers the world has ever seen may well grate on the nerves of our loved one. And of course, that friction may develop into a raging forest fire that could drive a wedge between even the most committed of couples. And these types of things, the comment that becomes a row, the row that becomes a fight, the fight that becomes the German invasion of Poland, always look worse from the outside.

Lindsey, 30, Crewe, Lecturer.

"Well, the four of us were going to Nottingham, you know, to see friends we know who moved there. Well, Kev would normally drive and I've got to say, he's really good, sensible, when we're going anywhere, especially if we've got other people with us. Well, the thing was that Kev was already down south. He's in sales and had been in Birmingham so it was easier for him to meet us there. It's not a problem, Ellen tells me, John will drive. Well, that was great. They'd pick me up straight from work and off we'd go. They were on time, had a load of wine and beer for the weekend. Well, I couldn't fault them, could I? So, off we go. And then it started. First of all, John drove like a maniac. I'm talking speed, I'm talking right up the back end of the car in front, overtaking without indicating, swearing, gesturing at other drivers. It was pretty scary but it was a favour. Well, I'm not going to complain, am I? The thing is, I can see Ellen getting more and more wound up. Not verbally, but she's darting him these looks, and he's seeing her, but just not paying attention. Then every time a song comes on he likes, he turns the volume up and she just snaps it back down, saying 'I am talking' even when she wasn't. So he carries on driving but now he's doing everything *more*. You know? Closer to the cars in front, faster, louder, and then there's signs clearly saying the motorway is cutting down to one lane and to stay left. Well, he just ploughs on in the outside lane, and cuts all these other people up, and he's got this real arrogant look on his face, and then she loses it with him and she is just screaming, 'John! John!

John!' over and over again. Well, I'm thinking that he just can't concentrate with that going on, and I'm thinking that she's forgotten I'm in the back. Seriously, every time he accelerates, she shrieks at him, every time he brakes, she howls. I wish he had been doing it on purpose, because if he had, it would have been the work of an evil genius.

I sit in the back, no choice but to watch this ridiculous scene going on in the front seats like it was a tennis match played out on the back of a lorry driving at a hundred and ten miles an hour! So what am I meant to do? Ask him to slow down and drive sensibly because it is clearly freaking Ellen out? Yeah, right! Well, I do what I think is the right thing and quietly open a bottle of wine. By the time we get there I don't care anymore and their fighting, well screaming, is going over my head. The last hour of the journey was a blur but I made sure Kev swore to me he would drive each and every time in the future. The worst thing was that I'm not sure that John even knew his driving had induced Ellen's mental state even when she informed him in front of us all that he'd be sleeping on the floor!"

The question that simply has to be considered is whether Ellen was more angry with John's driving or whether it was his ignorant bliss that had driven her to breaking point. I am sure this is something considered often by Ellen as she keeps the bed warm all by herself, and not for a single moment by John as he sleeps like a baby on the floor that really isn't that uncomfortable, after all.

Actually, the real question is whether the answer would have any impact on either John's driving or his behaviour. Many of the women reading this will have already made their minds up that, no, change was not in the offing, and that no matter how many nights John would spend sleeping on the floor, there was very little hope for the future of the relationship and Ellen should break away now while she still had the chance. I say many as opposed to all because there are the few women out there for whom her partner's lack of driving skills is not a deal breaker. Clearly such an enlightened way of thinking can only have been developed by the type of woman who is truly devoted to her man, no matter what his habits.

Gloria, 68, Retired, Swansea.

"Now, see, he hadn't been driving for years, because, let's face it, we didn't go that far, but when he realises that he can have a car through the Social, like, because he's on Disability, he thinks it's the best thing since sliced bread. Now, I'm not saying he was a bad driver and that, but, well, when he was driving proper last time, there weren't as many cars about, and I think all the cars now frightened him a bit. Not that he'd ever admit it, like, or that I'd ever say anything, but he was very cautious, slow like. And he used to think that as long as he waved his hand out of the window, signalling to other drivers to move over or even stop, then it was always his right of way. Roundabout, traffic lights, junctions, he'd wave until he made eye contact and then kind of raise his palm to them, and you could see the fear in their eyes as they braked and he just pulled out. Never had an accident, mind you, fair play. Bloody cold in the winter though, with his window open all the time. Now, it's not worth falling out over though, is it? His licence expires in six months."

So how far does a man have to get his driving wrong to incur the full wrath of a lady like Gloria? Let's assume that bumps, scrapes and accidents are off the table. Those things happen for a whole host of reasons and would, we hope, for the most part, result in sympathy rather than resentment, and if it is completely the man's fault then even the harshest of women would know that he will give himself far more of a hard time than she ever could. It is more likely to be stubbornness, shoving aside suggestions or superior stupidity that will suggest a slide towards relationship snags-ville. Or simply being simple. Something like this:

Sarah, 38, Lecturer, Aberystwyth.

"I know motorway driving is different. I accept that. It takes a whole different range of skills from city or rural driving. But some things about motorway driving are fairly obvious. You'd think, right? Owen is a good driver. Safe driver. I've never felt like I've got to crawl into the glove box to ensure my safety. So I ask him to drive me to Chepstow where I'm giving a presentation, and I don't want to be exhausted when I get there, and of course, because he is a good guy, he says yes. Now

Aberystwyth to Chepstow is an awkward route. It's country driving down to Swansea, and then it's straight along the M4. Owen's never done the drive before, so he asks my dad for some advice. He wasn't embarrassed to ask, so I remember it.

"Yes, join the motorway at Swansea and get off on Junction 23," Dad tells him and then laughs. "If you go over the big bridge, you've gone too far."

Owen nods, taking it all very seriously. So the next day we head off and all is going well. Once we get on the motorway, I kind of doze off and Owen seems fine, confident enough. Well, I wake up just as we're driving around Newport.

I panic a bit. "Owen, did you come off the motorway at Junction 23?"

He nods.

"Did you see the sign for Chepstow?"'

He shakes his head.

"I think you came off the wrong exit," I suggest.

He's not having it. "No, no, no," he insists. "We joined on Junction 49, and your dad says we exit after Junction 23, so I counted off each exit, one two, three, four...and when I'd got to 23 I turned off. Just like your dad said. Before I came to the big bridge. And there was no bridge in sight"

I wasn't going to fall out with him over his bizarre driving maths, but he just wouldn't listen, and by the time he did, I was late. Then I did have a quiet word with him."

At least the worst that Owen could be accused of was a little naivety and actually listening *too* well. The really stupid would do something more obvious. Something more arrogant. Something more man-like.

Kate, 45, Housewife, Ipswich.

"We're driving to his boss's house for dinner. He's never been there before, and we're approaching a t-junction. The Sat-Nav is telling us time and time again '*At the end of the road, turn left.*' He comes to a halt, looks left and right. The fancy woman tells us again to go left. He shakes his head and indicates right. "I'm sure it's this way," he says. We were an hour late. He still blames the Sat-Nav. I still blame him."

For all of man's mistakes when manoeuvring his motor, it is when he is in the passenger seat that he is most likely to earn himself three points on his licence and a heavy fine from his wife or girlfriend. It seems that a man in the passenger seat, being driven to his destination by a woman, is basically incapable of keeping his mouth shut. And the words, initially constructed inside the cerebral cortex as positive, life affirming supportive sentences, exit the mouth as a barbed and belligerent barrage of blurb. Basically, bull that's going to land us in the shit.

Matt, 28, Journalist, Wirral.

"Maybe I should just keep my mouth shut. Maybe I should. But it's not like I claim to be the greatest driver in the world, but at least when I was driving I felt safe, and whoever is in the car with me felt safe too. I'm sorry but when she's driving, I do not feel safe at all. Christ, she drives up to roundabouts faster than she joins the motorway, and then she brakes really hard, really late, and I am sure we're going to end up sliding across the road, getting munched by some massive truck."

Matt's partner, Sally, cannot hold back

anymore. She has sat stock still as Matt made his opening comments. She's not reacted to his gesticulating or the wide-eyed way in which he has tried to convey the fear he apparently feels when she is driving. However, as soon as he pauses to draw breath, she pounces. It is not so much what she has to say but the way she says it. Short, sharp and terse. With an overtone of 'You are in trouble.'

Sally, 27, Classroom Assistant, Wirral.

"Have I ever crashed? Have you?"

Matt fails to take the hint but instead sees her comment as a challenge. There is the distinct possibility that Sally has left her questions hanging there like bait. Matt does not let her down.

Matt, 28, Journalist, Wirral.

"Look, that's not the point. You drive too close to the cars in front, you never look ahead. Never."

"It's like if the road narrows, she'll never think that maybe it's her that should wait to merge, her that should be polite. No. She just goes. And even though the other car has stopped or pulled over or, more often the way she drives, reverses to clear the road for her, she never says thanks. Never flashes her lights or raises her hand. It's like she thinks she rules the road. I swear that I spend half the time when she is driving sat there with my jaw dropped because I can't believe what she's doing. And her lack of concentration is terrifying. She'll be looking sideways, telling me to look at the cute dog as the lights ahead have changed to red and our lane will be filling up with stopped cars. The worst thing is that if I say anything, all I get is her yelling that she saw them, but I know she hasn't, and the only reason she has is because I've had to shout at her. Mind you, I'm not the only one who feels like this. All my mates say their girlfriends can't drive either."

Sally shakes her head. Matt has nothing else to say. He has a look on his face that says, with confidence, that he has said it all. Sally glances at him and bites her top lip. She raises her eyebrows at him, a look that asks if it is now her turn to speak. He nods, but there is a glint in his eye that tells her that he believes she has nothing to contribute. He has no idea that he has already taken her bait and that he's about to be reeled in.

Sally, 27, Classroom Assistant, Wirral.

"Thanks for answering my question, by the way, but what the hell?"

"Let *me* give you *my* angle of *his* behaviour when I'm driving. Perhaps it will explain why I'm such a nervous driver. Right, first of all, if my foot ever, and I really do mean ever, is applied to the accelerator with anything other that minimal pressure, his hand darts up and he grabs hold of that little handle at the top of the door. He thinks I don't see him but I do. His knuckles are so white it's like he's on a rollercoaster. If I need to brake then his feet piston up and down like he's the one controlling the car, and I'll be honest and say it is massively distracting. Look, maybe I do brake late, but half the time it's because he's putting me off. It's the questions too, the constant stream of questions that tell me he thinks I'm a terrible driver. 'Are you in fifth gear?' 'Have you seen the whatever?' You know? It's just ridiculous. I reckon that half the time I've driven us somewhere, by the time we arrive I am a complete bag of nerves, and we end up having a fight. And it's not just what he's said to me but the fact that it carries on and everyone has to hear that I've nearly killed us ten times over on the way. So you're probably wondering why he doesn't drive all the time? Right? If I am so bad why doesn't he drive all the time? Are you going to answer that one, Matt? You can answer my earlier question at the same time if you like."

Sally sits back in her chair with a very smug look on her face. She's got Matt on the end of her hook and she's happily let him squirm around for a while, possibly even let him believe that this was a situation he could extract himself from, but now she's gone for the kill. Matt looks pale, beaten. He's truly cemented his place in the dog house. After about five minutes of huffing and puffing with a few desperate looks thrown in, the truth comes to light.

Matt, 28, Journalist, Wirral.
"My car's in the garage. I crashed it a few weeks ago. I didn't stop in time at a roundabout."

So it would appear that man would be advised to reserve judgment on his partner's driving skills if he wishes to maintain a happy life. Unfortunately, he cannot help himself. The words are probably out of his mouth quicker than she can reverse off the drive without checking if anything is coming. The problem may of course be something genetic, handed down from their fathers and from their fathers' fathers. Back in the day, men did *all* the driving. Simple as that. Often the lady would choose to sit in the back of the car, even when there were no other passengers, so the transition to women being considered equals in the driver's seat has not been easy for men to assimilate. But voicing our frustrations, constantly, is not the way forward. *That* is for sure.

Under Wearing Well.

On the whole, men have terrible fashion sense. Well, not so much terrible fashion *sense* but terrible fashion *appropriateness*. How many men think it is okay to wear their favourite football team's offensively coloured third kit to the pub on a first date? Or a rugby shirt to Sunday lunch with the grandparents? Or a t-shirt that reads 'It ain't gonna suck itself' on the day they are going to ask their girlfriend's dad for her hand in marriage? The list of such fashion faux pas is endless. There is a temptation to leave a little box here for the lady's in the audience to write their worst such moment and, of course, for the lads to note their *best*! Instead, ladies, take a moment to remind your man of a time when you've wanted to send him home to get changed. And men, just keep it shut. Please.

Keep it shut because, men, you think it is okay to bypass a dress shirt and wear a printed t-shirt instead. You think it is okay to wear the same pair of pants for days on end after you have owned then for years on end. You think that your y-fronts are the height of genital fashion. You think that those holes in your briefs are for vital ventilation. You think that wearing your wife's bra is the funniest thing since you took a photo of your pooh and showed it to the vicar on your wedding day. You think that because you don't mind where you put her thong that she shouldn't mind where you stick your grotty boxer shorts. You think all these things, yes. It just surprises the girls that you actually go beyond thinking them. No wonder women are generally accepted as being the fairer sex.

Women take longer to get ready for a reason. The end result is undoubtedly more elegant and polished than anything any man will ever achieve. They take pride in how they look. They carefully apply the makeup and just the right amount of a carefully selected perfume. They do this to make us men happy. They do not do it, as many men have suggested, because they are ugly and they smell bad!

They select clothes that suit the situation. They take the time to match shoes, accessories, jewellery, the hair, and they end up with an ensemble that is a sum greater than its individual parts.

Alternatively, your average man would prefer

to be told what to wear. Maybe that is why men are comfortable in sports kits. There is no need to stand out, in fact, it is better to be a part of the crowd, like wearing a school uniform; it allows him to blend in without having to make too much effort. The same could be said for formal dinners where the old penguin outfit is the one and only option. Every man thinks he looks good in a tuxedo, mainly because they've not had think too hard to get it right. But even with such a simple option, some men can still be very, very unfashionably wrong.

Rory, 25, Former Boyfriend of a Barrister, London.

"Elaine was a few years older than me, and she was a career solicitor, or whatever, so she always had to go to these fancy dinners and corporate events, and I'd always been able to weasel out of going. But she'd won this award thing, so I'd finally had to go, right? She gives me detailed, and I mean detailed, notes on what I've got to wear, and I go out and hire the lot. Patent leather shoes. These black trousers with a silky stripe down the outside. A black dinner jacket. A properly starched shirt and a dickie bow. It cost more to hire it than it cost me to buy the best suit I own! So I'm getting ready, and the tie is one of those do it yourself-ers, and I'm making a mess of it. So I run out to the shop to get, well, I didn't know, but a clip-on bow tie or something, and I pass a shop, and in the window they've got a t-shirt printed up to look like a dress shirt. Well, I go in and it's only three-dimensional, isn't it? It's got a proper collar, the bow tie is all fluffed up, the shirt has even got some ruffles down the front. Okay, if I'd not been starting to run a bit late and had panic setting in, maybe I'd have taken a few minutes and realised I was being stupid, but I wasn't thinking that far ahead. I had to be in a taxi to pick her up at quarter to eight, and I was bang on time. I'd have gotten away with it, too, if I'd not taken my jacket off when the dancing started. She dumped me in the taxi on the way home. It wasn't even 11p m."

To be fair, bad fashion sense is not really something that will land a man in trouble. Most women would rather be the ones that look the more glamorous, the more cultured, the more classy of the couple. They may even see improving his sartorial elegance as a project. However, they do want their advice to be heeded, especially if the phrase 'I don't think that is suitable' is included. Let's take it for granted that most men, if their wife or girlfriend told them that their favourite Megadeath t-shirt wasn't really the best thing to wear to a wedding, would go and get changed. You see, the man who receives this bit of guidance should have the common sense to take the approach that his loved one is simply looking out for him and is making sure he does not make a fool of himself. He is happy that she just wants him to have a frontal façade of feminine friendly fashion. What he has no idea of is that she expects the clothes that no one else but she will see to be immaculate too. We are of course referring to the most unimportant part of any man's life, and that is his underwear.

A lady will take an incredible amount of pride in how she looks underneath her business suit. She will want to impress as much when she steps out of her cocktail dress as she did when she was wearing it. She will take the time to ensure that every single one of her man's senses is titillated and teased when she leads him to the bedroom, and will go that one step further to ensure she is a feast for his eyes as much as everything else. She wishes, however, that just once her man would make just an ounce of effort in the erotica department too.

Mel, 25, Call Centre Manager, Derby.

"Jamie was hot, no doubt about it. I got his shirt off and discovered he had the body of an underwear model. I swear. I was completely impressed. We're kissing and I fell back on the bed. God, this is embarrassing, but that's how it went, and he stands over me and slowly undoes his belt, and he's got a button fly instead of a zip, and he knows what he's doing as he slowly undoes them one at a time until he finally lets his jeans fall to his ankles."

Mel stops and shakes her head. There is look of distant disappointment in her eyes.

"Sorry. It's just that he's wearing these horrible white things. They weren't Y-fronts as such, but they were briefer than some of my briefs. And there's a...there's a luminous yellow stain dried in at the front. Thank God he got them off damn quick because as hot as he was, he'd killed the moment right there."

The problem lies in that a man does not see his

under pants as a tool of the trade. He simply sees them as a necessary item of clothing that fulfils a particular task. It is very much a case of function over form. Could it be that man's reluctance to invest in a good pair of underpants is simply left down to the fact that they do not actually *expect* anyone to see them apart from themselves? Maybe so, but it would also appear that even when they think there may be some near nudity, men are not really committed to the cause. Why spend all that cash on the same boxer shorts that David Beckham wears when the rest of the package does not match up? Dressing mutton like lamb comes to mind. However, whereas a man may argue that picking up a pack of twenty budget briefs from the local supermarket means they have more cash for a fancy dinner out, most women would say that they would happily take a nice meal and a little bit more in terms of male genital hygiene. And, probably, even if a girlfriend or a wife tried to subtly hint that the issue is progressing to a problem, most men still would not change a single thing.

Nathan, 28, Healthcare Provider, Newcastle.
"Well, man, the thing is, like, I work hard all week and then on the weekend, I just likes to take it easy, like. If we're not going out,

like, then I won't have a shower. I just can't be bothered. In work, like, I'm so obsessed with cleanliness so it's nice to have a break from it, like. See man, I'll stick me tracksuit on and that's me set for the day. Half the time I'll fall asleep in front of the telly, and when I wake up the next day, like, well there's no bother putting something else on. Now me missus, man, she's on me case about it all the time and I tells her, like, when we go out I'll get washed and shaved and changed, but if we're doing nowt then I just like to slob. I won't lie to you, I might wear me pants all weekend, and to be honest, like, it makes no difference to me. Saves on the washing, like, innit? See, saving the planet me. Reducing me carbon foot print. Tell her that, though? Apparently I've got to be washed and clean and wearing *clean boxers* before she'll go near me! Who is she like? The Queen?"

There is a concern not only about the regularity of underwear being changed but also about the fact that men tend to cling to their unmentionables longer than the clothing is capable of clinging to them.

Craig Jones and Siôn James

Tracy, 33, Personal Assistant, Portsmouth.

"No, no, no, my problem isn't cleanliness. Fair play to him, he'd change them three times a day if the weather, or exercise or what have you, called for it. What I'm bothered about is that when he changes them, each subsequent pair will be older and more threadbare than the last. He just will not throw them out. I reckon I can see the elastic on the waistband of at least half of them. He's got this one pair of Calvin Klein's. Just the one pair, obviously, and he's worn them to death. You know they are meant to be quite tight? Well, without being nasty, he's put on a few pounds since he bought them and they are now verging on being baggy on him. They've lost all of their, you know, what's the word?"

Tracy gestures with her hands and puckers up her mouth in a way that makes me think of the word 'suction' and I guess that, while not what she actually means, it's the best word for her concern.

"Like I said, half of them, the elastic is visible, while the other half...umm...well, his skin is visible. His backside is visible. I'm not sure he's got a pair that is fully 'new' looking. Even when I've bought him some, for Christmas or birthdays, he doesn't bring them into circulation. I'm not sure what he's waiting for. Okay, so maybe I'd be picky if I said it was a turn off, but is it a turn on? No! I guess if I walked in and he'd covered the bed in rose petals and was lying there in his holey underpants, I don't think my first reaction would be to leap on him. Well, not unless he'd finally had those Calvin Klein's taken in."

Maybe it is not the average man's fault that he struggles to motivate himself when it comes to underwear purchases. At the end of the day the selection is fairly basic. Boxers, briefs, trunks. Variations therein. If food was all about meat and two veggies then there'd be no such thing as celebrity chefs. Imagine that!

But for women there are all sorts of options. Thongs, shorts, hipsters, satin, lace, cotton. The list is endless. The combinations are more complex than a Swiss bank vault. Add bras, tights, stockings, and suddenly, putting on the most basic of clothing can become a hobby in itself. Matching colours, styles and fabrics to suit the moment. What equivalent has a man got? A grubby vest to match his tidy whities? Could this be the reason that a man, while having no interest in his own underwear, can develop such an obsession with hers? And why, if left on his own for long enough, he may even go as far as to experiment in trying on some of her more flamboyant garments.

Shane, 38, Civil Servant, Exeter.

"I was getting dressed after a shower, and the garment was there on the bed, and to be honest, the thing had always pretty much intimidated me, so I picked it up and had a proper look. Wow! What a contraption! Such a simple word, *bra*, but come on? Those things defy gravity. What did the old ad say? *Lift and separate?* And yet it felt so soft, too. Like I said, wow! And, yes, of course I know it is childish and inappropriate *now*, but at the time, well, I just wanted to see what it was like, so I slipped my arms through the straps and tried it on. I couldn't see the harm in it. It's not like I did it up or anything, and Paula's actually agreed since that I hadn't stretched it or anything, so I still think that if I've not bust it...ha-ha...bust, get it? Anyway, sorry, I made myself giggle there, but like I was saying, I didn't damage it.

I just admired myself in the mirror for too long, I guess, and when Paula came in she went nuts. Called me weird, told me I was disrespectful. She gave me grief for weeks, but I still don't see the harm in it."

Shane's fiancée, Paula, is much clearer on the issues that Shane should have kept abreast of.

Paula, 35, Dental Hygienist, Exeter.

"Well first of all, it cost me a comparative fortune. Men just don't realise how important, and therefore how expensive, a good bra is. Second of all, he was leaning forward toward the mirror, squeezing his ever more flaccid chest muscles together, trying to create his own 'cleavage shot.' And finally, he called it my 'over the shoulder boulder holder.' And he wonders why I called him weird and disrespectful! What should I expect from him next? Going on X Factor dressed up as Cher?"

A man's ability to land himself in hot water with his partner's underwear stretches beyond a bizarre fascination in seeing how he will look wearing it. It will even impinge upon other areas of his life where he is likely to get on her wrong side. Such as shopping. Let's face it, most men would rather avoid clothes shopping, and yet the lure of earning good behaviour credits draws us into an arena where we know we have no place. We may start with an enthusiastic rush of endorphins, but before long, one dress merges into the next, and before long, we simply find ourselves nodding our agreement that the next one looks better than the previous until, of course, we end up back in the very first shop as she pays for the very first dress she tried on. Five hours ago. When we told her it looked fantastic first time around.

Of course, we try to keep our mouths shut. We try not to make a sarcastic comment. We often fail. But even if this minefield is sidestepped and we think we are making all the right sounds, she ups the odds of a meltdown by suggesting that she needs some new knickers. But still we go. Remember, we are trying to say that we are the most attentive of men on the planet. We are probably still trying to make up for some previous misdemeanour. And instead of excusing ourselves and going to buy DVDs, CDs or books, we tag along and stand there, uncomfortable, desperately trying to avoid eye contact with any other human beings in the store, trying even harder not to stare too hard at any of the more risqué garments, and for a while we are doing okay. Then it happens. They choose to leave us alone for a few minutes. They know the risk but they do it anyway, and by the time they emerge from the changing rooms, we have done something that will have them storming for the exit.

Gemma, 26, Barmaid, Leeds.

"So we're in *that* shop. You know the one I mean? The one that sells sexy underwear as well as other *stuff*? The *toys* and stuff? Well I was expecting him to be a bit of an idiot, if truth be known, but initially he proved me wrong. Okay, he looked out of place, that goes without saying, and he's hardly looking at the shelves and he certainly hasn't looked up to see what I'm taking into the changing cubicle with me. But I'm not too bothered because I guess I'm already thinking that it'll be a nice surprise for him when he sees me wearing it. Because he's earned a bit of a treat. He's driven me into town, he's spent ages giving me his advice, and he's said some really sweet things about how I looked in some of the clothes I tried on. Even the things that I *knew* weren't great. But he's been dead patient and he stands

there like a statue, head down, like a little boy
sent to stand outside the head teacher's office.
So I try the stuff on, decide what I want, and
then when I come out it is like 'Oh, my God,'
because he's now stood by one of the displays
of thongs, and he's picked one up and he's
holding the string bit between his fingers, and
with this manic grin on his face he's
pretending to floss his teeth with it! Okay, so
it's not really close to his mouth but it's close
enough for the girl behind the counter to
giggle behind her hand. God knows who else
saw him! So I dump what I was going to buy
on the counter and leave, and he hasn't even
seen me. I had to phone him to get him to
follow me out. And he still doesn't get why
he's never seen me wearing the new sexy
underwear I was going to get for him."

So, it is likely that a man's misbehaviour
around his missus' unmentionables, and of course in
regard to the maintenance of his own, will be the least
of his worries. For the most part, although irritating, it
would be a major shock if a man ended up on the
scrap heap simply for not dispatching his pants there
in the first place. However, it is really that these

actions are not that serious, or is it that we somehow contrive to give our women far more to worry about? I think that is one question where both male and female readers will agree. Yes, men can find much better ways to screw things up than having a pee stain on their pants or flossing with a g-string! And, if such a thing is a *possibility*, you can trust a man to turn it into a *probability*.

Take Brett. He's a professional man. He's in a fully committed relationship. He has not been in the dog house with his girlfriend for over three years. He hasn't even had more than four beers since he vomited on her dog. He listens to her fashion advice, and has learnt just when he should nod and just when he should keep his mouth shut. Some might say that Brett had it made. Within a two week period, he, of course, blew it. All because he decided that wearing his underpants was a completely boring past-time and that the opportunity to introduce a brand new challenging game to his and his partner's life was too much to resist.

Brett, 26, Sales Manager, Gloucester.

"I call it pantsing. Now I know there's a whole other practical joke that's called pantsing where you pull your mate's trousers down in public so everybody sees the old twig and two berries. But everyone's done that one, right? It's like such a childish way to behave. Now my version of it is completely different and far more entertaining. The idea came to me one night when I was getting undressed for bed. The t-shirt came off. I balled it up and shot a basket into the washing. The jogging trousers came off. I made it two shots from two. Then the underpants came off just as Rosie came out of the bathroom and shook her head at me. So instead of going for the hat trick, I pulled the pants down over her head! She went mental for about thirty seconds and then saw the funny side of it. "You got me," she said. "But that's enough. Don't do it again." And in that second she turned it from a momentary bit of fun to a challenge. How many ways could I pants her? Did I award myself extra points if I'd just farted into said pants? What about if some pant material actually went inside her mouth? The opportunities were endless. It was just hilarious."

Rosie, 26, Annoyed, Gloucester.
"Oh, yeah. It was hilarious. About as

hilarious as anal rape! Do you know that in the middle of his pantsing spree I hardly slept? And you want to know why? Cos he'd leave his filthy, grotty underpants under my pillow. Because he'd wait until I was asleep and then reach under his own pillow and pull out the pair he'd been wearing all day and drape them over my face. It got to the point where I was twitchy as a nut job. If he wasn't in the room, I'd have my eyes on the door, permanently, to catch him sneaking in. We were in the cinema once and I thought I was safe, and he put his arm around me, and I actually remember thinking, 'This is nice, I don't have to worry about...' and that was as far as I got because he'd brought a pair of pants with him and laid them over my shoulder. He thought it was hysterical. I was sick in my mouth."

Brett, 26, Deep in the shit, Gloucester.

"That wasn't my best one though, was it? Best one, without a doubt, was when I hadn't pantsed Rosie in over a week. She'd been too good for me. Checked under the pillows, made sure my pants went straight into the washing machine, safely out of the bedroom. I just could not get a pair of pants over her head for love nor money. And it came to me in a flash of inspiration. One morning I left for work earlier than Rosie, took her spare car keys with me and pulled a pair of my used gym pants over her steering wheel. The text message I got from her twenty minutes later was the best, most abusive text message ever. Apparently all the neighbours heard her shriek and throw them into the road. So she had to pick them up and take them inside. My pants that is, not the neighbours. So not only have I scored with the pantsing but also with did it in front of witnesses. In-Spir-Ation."

Rosie, 26, Raging, Gloucester.
"Inspiration? You are a fucking idiot."

As are, it seems, most men.

A Drinking Demon.

Due to the drinking culture that is very much a part of society today, a man can be defined by the amount of pints he can put away on a night out. This of course can lead to all manner of ills and a great number of poor behaviours that are simply shameful. Put a group of men together and, unfortunately, they will encourage each other to consume more and more ale. The end result is often not good. However, we have no interest in the type of man who would blow his week's wages on gallon after gallon of lager. We don't want to discuss the type of man for whom alcohol is an excuse for aggressive and nasty traits to come to the fore. And we certainly have no time for any man who uses *being drunk* as an excuse for where his penis ends up. You see, a man needs none of these attributes to end up in the wrong after a few pints with the lads, and you can be certain that, if the opportunity presents itself, beer is yet another tool that allows a man to become nothing more than a tool himself.

Alcohol will impact upon a man's personality in many ways. For some it brings out a seldom seen extrovert who is fun and entertaining and whose wife or girlfriend may find difficult to control. For others it may burrow deep into their unconscious and manifest itself in ways that they have no chance of keeping under wraps or even remembering. Drink will, for certain, remove inhibitions. The problems come when these controls are there for a reason. Like to ensure social norms. You see, a drunk man will not hesitate to urinate wherever he sees fit. If he can see at all, of course. A drunk man will embark upon adventures that his staid and button-down personality would not dare consider when sober. Unfortunately, often these daring deeds when drink driven are done while fast asleep. Worse, however, is to come when the drunk man simply will not see that enough is enough and wishes to continue his merriment later and later into the night, despite all bars and high street shops, being closed. And for others, well, it may just send them to sleep. Because of course, they can't do any harm then. Can they?

Gloria, 68, Retired, Swansea.

"Now what I will say is this, he was never a 'boozer' and he never ever raised his hand to me. It wasn't his nature sober, and beer never changed him in that way, see, fair play. But I'll tell what it did do, and that was to make him flake out. Just like that. No warning and he'd be gone. The thing is, see, back when we were a bit younger, it used to be the done-thing to have house parties. Pubs weren't like they are now, see, so you'd invite your friends over, lay on some food, and everyone would bring a bottle. I used to love it. All the men would be playing cards and smoking, and us women would be in the kitchen, catching away, like. Well, you could bet your housekeeping that around about half past ten, he'd crash out and he wasn't fussy where. On the settee, on the floor, he'd be out like a light. Now that by itself wasn't a problem, I'll tell you, but it's what he used to do when he *was* asleep that used to embarrass me. He'd be flat out and then he'd decide he'd want to change position, and the first thing he'd do would be to throw one of his arms up in the air and then as he rolled over he'd shout out. Nothing you could properly make out but it was bloody loud, see? He didn't half terrify the heck out of the nearest person. And when the arm landed, well, it was like skittles. Bottles, cans, glasses, the lot would go flying. One time it landed on one of my friend's breasts! Poor girl! It got to the point the other men used to bet how long it would take him to shout out with his big, stupid windmill arm. Silly bugger used to deny he'd even been asleep."

Most women would kill for a partner who just wanted to wave his arm around and shout a little bit while asleep. For some, the issue is much more serious and ends up in sleepless nights, worried about where her partner is going to end up even though he is lying on the bed, comatose, right next to her.

Caroline, 30, GP Practice Manager, Belfast.

"Oh my God. It was mental. Like seriously mental. The first thing I knew about it was the following morning at breakfast, but it was absolutely mental. My sister and her husband run a pub, and Simon and I went to stay with them for the weekend. Simon and my brother in law, Pat, get on great, but when they get on the beer together they can be a bit mental. So on Friday night, me and Alex leave them to it so we can have a proper catch up. So we have a good night and after Pat's staff had closed up, we all go off to bed. Simon's all right, slurring a bit, but all right really. He tried to get into bed in his jeans and his shoes, but he listened when I told him to get undressed, and then, as far as I know, we're both off to the land of nod. Breakfast the next morning, Alex and Pat burst out laughing every time they look at Simon, and he looks well sheepish, so I ask what's going on. "Nothing," he tells me. "Bollocks," says my sister, who never swears. "What's going on," I ask again, and this time Pat has to leave the room, he's laughing that much.

I'm starting to think the pair of them are mental. Simon is staring so deep into his coffee that I think he actually wants to climb down into the cup. Alex gets a grip and starts to relate what's gone on. Apparently, she and Pat were fast asleep when she gets woken up by a noise. She feels Pat stir next to her so she gives him a nudge. "Listen to that rain," she tells him, and he sits bang upright. "That's not rain." He points across the room to the window where Simon is stood, having pulled the curtains wide open, and he's peeing up against the glass. Alex says she shouted, "What are you doing?" and now she cracks up so much she can't even breathe let alone speak. I swear she'd fall to the floor if she didn't have the kitchen table to hold her up. "What are you doing?" she repeats, completely out of breath. And then pat comes back in the room, tears rolling down his face as he tells me, "And Simon tells us, calm as you like..." The pair of them can't stop laughing. Pat's voice is high pitched when he squeaks out the words that came out of Simon's mouth. "I'm having a wee!" and then he finished up and walked out, I'm guessing he came back to bed. Can you imagine how I felt? I bring him away for a weekend and my sister has to end up cleaning his piss from off their bedroom floor? The next visit? He was only allowed two pints a night."

One has to wonder whether the problem lies in Simon's nocturnal urinations or the fact that he got caught doing it by someone else. Is it somehow worse that other people know his dirty little secret? Had it happened in the sanctuary of her own home, would Caroline have shared this event to her friends and family? Would she have spilt it to her sister if he'd just done it in their room, even? The probable answer is *no* because unlike men, women would rather avoid any embarrassing stories about their loved ones. However, there are occasions when the lady in the relationship will let something slip. And even then, obviously, it will still be the man's fault.

Roger, 27, Musician, Luton.

"Martin's my best mate and has been for years, and after we got married we used to go away with the wives a few times a year. We were in the Lake District. Penny and I were on our way to bed on our second night. Martin and Carol had gone up from the bar about fifteen minutes before us, and we had to walk past their room to get to our room. We'd not had loads to drink: a couple of bottles of wine with dinner and maybe a pint or two after. Well, as we walk past their door, Penny grabs hold of my arm and stops me, putting her finger to her lips to shut me up.

Carol must have been stood right on the other side of the door because her voice was crystal clear. "Martin, Martin?" she calls. "I'm putting the chain on the door tonight, in case you try to get out." We hear the security chain being latched in place and then Martin's voice calls, "Yeah, that's a good idea. Just in case." Now, we're stood there, mouths wide open, not sure whether we should be laughing or banging on their door asking for an explanation. We managed to hold off until breakfast when we asked what was going on. "Nothing," says Martin and shoots Carol a look that she clearly sees and chooses to ignore. "Night before last, action man here tries to climb up the wardrobe. I wake up and his little naked bum is wiggling in the air, and I think he's going to fall so I call out to him and he staggers back down. I think he's coming to bed and instead he walks for the door, and we'd not put the chain on. Stupid sod would have been in the corridor naked if I hadn't grabbed hold of him." I guess it's no surprise that Penny's first question was "You must be so proud?" to which Carol gives Martin this death stare. "See how you embarrass me?" Poor Martin just sits there and shrugs. He's not said a word but he's the one in the shit!"

Sometimes a man does not need sleep to bring

on an alcohol induced walkabout. It would seem that booze may have secret regenerative powers that encourage men to turn into athletes of Olympic proportions. Well, at least in their own heads. However much they may be encouraged to run, leap and jump by their male mates, it is very seldom that such activity would be rewarded with a gold medal by the long suffering girlfriend, no matter how many personal bests are bettered.

Mark, 28, Chartered Surveyor, Aberdeen.

"Now you see, it all started off so well. We'd planned this long weekend in Dublin for the rugby international. Scotland against Ireland. It wasn't like we expected to win but we knew it was going to be a great time. And we'd played a blinder. The four of us lads, we'd agreed to take the girls and booked it all without them knowing so it was a nice surprise and we were all heroes in our own households. The girls, they've got no interest in the match, so they're going to do the whole shopping and dinner thing on Saturday, and we've earned our passes out, but on Friday the eight of us go for an early dinner and then out on the town. The plan was to take it easy, but we run into a bunch of Irish rugby fans, and they're as friendly as you'd expect, so we have a few too many. Or rather, us boys do and Tony, well, Tony is lethal on the booze. He don't drink that often, so he was half cut after dinner let alone in the pub, and I see his missus, Donna, having a quiet word with him, but he's not paying any attention. In the end, my girlfriend says to me that it's probably for the best that we all head home, and I have to agree with her. The big day out for us lads is yet to come so none of us really want to be hung-over on match day. It takes a while but we finally get Tony to say bye and leave his last pint behind. Look, maybe I should have kept a closer eye on him when we got outside, but I didn't expect him to just run off!"

Tony's wife, Donna, doesn't agree with Mark. She vehemently blames her husband for what came next.

Donna, 29, Banker, Aberdeen.

"I'd warned him in advance not to get wasted, and I warned him through the night a few times, too, but the arse just didn't want to listen. When Mark finally got his pint off of him and we headed out, Tony decided he wanted the night to carry on so he sprints across the road towards this bright fronted place. Seriously, he dodges taxis like he was a rugby player and he starts banging on the front door, asking to be let in. The rest of us finally catch up with him and we ask what he's playing at.

"They won't let me in," he shouts, attracting the attention of everyone around us, and people are virtually pointing as they laugh at him. "Let me in," he shouts again, properly banging on the glass door.

"They're not going to let you in," I tell him. "It's a Top Shop!" Not fazed at all, he shrugs and pulls a face. His bottom lip goes out like a little child, and before any of us can react, he unzips his trousers, turns around and starts to pee against the door. He's peeing against the door of a Top Shop in Dublin! There's no stopping him, but at least the lads formed a cordon around him so no one could see. The fool was lucky not to get arrested. He finishes up, but it's running back, all over *his* shoes, all over *everyone's* shoes! He looks across the road and sees the pub we've just been in and, thank God, just as he's going to make a break for it, a couple of the lads grab hold of him and start to frogmarch him back to our hotel. I let him go to the match the next day, and have his lads' night out, but his credit card? That came with me!"

Now why does a man have to get himself into alcohol related trouble in a hotel room or on the streets of a distant city when he can do himself, and his relationship, just as much harm in the comfort of his own home? Even though he should know every nook and cranny, there are still places that will inevitably trip the inebriated up and, more often that not, his good lady will be there to witness his misdemeanours. Possibly the biggest problem for a man who comes home drunk is not the fear of the wife waiting behind the door with a rolling pin in her hand but the simple fact that a sober wife will recall every detail the following day. And the one after that. And, you've guessed it, every single day until he does something so good that she has no alternative but to finally forget about it and put it to bed. Like she most likely had to do to him when he came home drunk.

Kerry, 30, Project Manager, Doncaster.

"Look, I don't mind if he has a night out. I don't mind if he gets wrecked. I don't mind if he can't remember a single thing the next morning as long as he gets himself home and doesn't puke in our bed. And more often than not he just goes to the pub down the road with one or two of his mates, which gives me a chance to have some of my friends over, sometimes it's his mates' wives, sometimes not.

This one night, Ronnie says he and Colin fancy a catch up and a pint, and Colin's wife, Vic, wants to pop round and see me. Lovely. Everyone's happy. Well, the boys are a bit later than we thought but, no worries, and when the front door opens they're a bit loud and lively, but again, no worries. Ronnie goes straight up the stairs to the loo, I guessed, and Colin comes into the living room. He's grinning like a Cheshire Cat. Vic gives him a dirty look, and all he does is laugh at her. For a moment, a really, really brief moment, I am smug. Ronnie would never do that to me. He knows his limits, he knows...and then I hear the bathroom door open and the house fills with the sound of thunder. *Thud. Thump, Thump. Thud. Thump. Thud.* Each subsequent impact coming louder and faster than the last. We all rush out into the hallway where Ronnie's lying facedown at the foot of the stairs.

"That hurt," he says and both he and Colin burst out laughing.

I help him to his feet and notice both of his elbows are bleeding, his chin is bleeding, one knee of his jeans is torn, there's blood on the floor. I can't be angry with him while he's hurt. I sit him on the bottom step as Vic and Colin make their embarrassed excuses and leave. The two boys are still giggling as I close the door behind them. I step over Ronnie and run up the stairs to get the first-aid kit from the bathroom. I pull the light switch and then all my sympathy goes down the toilet. He's peed all over the seat, all over the floor and he's not flushed. I grab the first-aid kit, but as I get halfway back down the stairs, and he's still laughing his head off. I lose it. I throw the little green bag at the back of his head, tell him to sort himself out, and I storm to bed. Lucky for him he didn't even attempt to join me. He could have slept on the floor as far as I cared, but when I got up the next morning, I see he'd taken care of his war wounds and cleaned the bathroom from floor to ceiling. I still stayed in a mood with him for a week, though. By the end of it he'd cooked every meal, washed every pot, and vacuumed twice a day. He's been very careful on the stairs since!"

Of course, drink can make us do the strangest things, actions which at the time seem so logical and matter of course that we are unable to see the need to change from the path that we are on and behave any differently. Take poor Abby as an example. Her brother and his best friend came to visit from Scotland, and Abby's husband was more than happy to take them out on a lads' night in Cardiff. Abby was delighted. She was pleased that her husband and brother were getting on so well. She hoped that special spouse, Steve, would also get on with Anthony, her brother, David's best friend. She had no reason to worry at all.

Abby, 29, Dietitian, Cardiff.

"I'd had a really busy week in work and to have two nights out in a row. It's really not me anymore, so when Steve said he'd take charge of Saturday evening, I was so pleased. He's a good husband. It's not like he's out every week so I thought it was good for him. And great that he actually wanted to spend some time with my brother and his mate. So I have a nice night in, watching Bridget Jones, and then I go off to bed. David was in the spare room and Anthony was on a blow up mattress in the study. I heard them come in, kind of, but they were all pretty considerate, and next thing I know, Steve is snuggling up to me but I'm already drifting back to sleep. Then I wake up because Steve is out of bed. He's stood by the bedroom door, completely naked, and then he goes out onto the landing. I listen, thinking he's gone to the loo, but when I don't hear the bathroom door open, I get up, put my dressing gown on, and go after him. I see that the study door is wide open and that there is light coming from under the bathroom door, so I'm a bit confused, and then I hear giggling from the study so I stick my head around the door, and there's Steve, wrapped up in the spare duvet on the blow up mattress. "What are doing?" I whisper. "That's for Anthony!" Well, all he does is laugh, so I grab hold of him, realising it must be Anthony in the bathroom and think that I need to get my naked husband back to bed quickly, and I manage to manhandle him back to our room just before the flush goes and the bathroom door opens. I close our bedroom door, thinking I'd just been in a cartoon where we'd just gotten away with something, and I turn to Steve, and now he's no longer naked but somehow is wearing a pair of jeans. "What are you getting dressed for?" I ask. "I found them," he slurs. "Found them where?" I ask, still half asleep but a fair bit more alert than my idiot husband. "They were in the study," he answers, as if it was the most obvious response in the world. And then it clicks. Steve has stolen Anthony's jeans. I wanted them all to get on, to bond, but not that bloody much! How do I explain that to my brother in the morning? "Sorry, David, my naked husband stole your friend's jeans in the middle of the night." Yeah, right!"

You see, a man does not need to be a thug, a drunk, an inconsiderate oaf or a savings spending waste of space to be an idiot. Ask any woman. Every single female on the planet will have a story that makes their man resemble the biggest buffoon alive. Unfortunately, the gent involved will either not be able to remember what went on so as to defend the accusations levelled at him, or he will be all too aware of what he did and open-heartedly acknowledge his short comings. Possibly most of the ones who know what they did wrong feign forgetfulness anyway. It would at least detract a little bit from their actions. Until the next time, at least.

Memoir of a Geezer

Now you may be wondering to yourself: "I wonder if the Geezer has ever gotten himself in trouble because of alcohol?" Well, the answer, pure and simple, is that of course he has. Time and time again. The only real difficulty with this topic is specifying just which incident best reflects his inability to ever be in the good books. There are a couple of issues to consider. Do we take an example from his youth when, if we are honest, we all, male or female, let booze get the better of us? Do we seek out a time in his single life when one too many cost him badly? Or do we go directly to the time when even he was getting it so right, he still, with just a few pints to blame, got it so, so wrong? The latter? Of course it's the latter!

Up and unders, downs and ups.

"Right, so the lads are on your back about going to Edinburgh for the Six Nations rugby match between Wales and Scotland, and you know, know as an absolute fact, that if you ask the wife if you can go, she is going to remind you that you swore the next trip away was going to be just the two of you and someplace romantic. How the Hell am I meant to pull this one off?

See, no matter how I can try to wrap this one up with whistles and bows, glitter and tinsel, as far as she is concerned, it is no better than polishing a turd. Me being the turd. And then it comes to me in a flash of what can only be heavenly inspiration. *We all take the girls.* Now, let's be honest, this going down well with the lads was not expected to be the actual outcome, but one by one they began to see the logic. Maybe I'm not the only one constantly on the verge of screwing everything up. Maybe it's like that behind their closed doors too. Maybe I'm the only one stupid enough to tell my mates about how downright whipped I am!

The problem is that it only takes one comment, a miniscule detail for the wheels to start to come off the worst laid plans of us men. "We've only got the four tickets," says Rhys, before applying the mind-numbing logic that makes us all fear for his ability to dress himself properly, let alone keep a wife happy. "And if the girls come, there'll be eight of us." He pauses again, as if for effect but, in fact, to give himself thinking time. "That means we don't have enough tickets for us all."

There is a collective sigh, but I've already spotted this misnomer and have got the answer ready and waiting. Now, let me just say that I hadn't expected to have to use my get-out-of-jail card with the lads. No, I didn't think I'd have to. The get-out-of-jail card was to use on the wife, when she, as she would, asked what was in it for her. "We tell them that we knew they'd not want to go to the match and that it gave them more time to go shopping!"

I was a genius. Fact. Stop the world now because I want to get off to meet my fans and let them remember where they were the day they met me! If I could have bottled that moment, the looks on the lads' faces, the awe with which they exalted me, then I could have made a fortune. And so it came to be that the night ended early and each of us departed with a pat on the back from the rest of comrades in arms, a wish of 'good luck' and a promise to text the end result as soon as possible. And of course it was then that the nerves kicked in. All this good promise could simple vanish into the ether if Rosie, she who was expecting a romantic weekend away, were to call me to rights and insist upon me delivering that which I was looking to get out of.

"Why now?" she says with a proper happy smile. I manage to keep my own smile under wraps until I'm in the bathroom alone, texting thumb going like the clappers, similar delirious replies pinging back in, and we know it is on and that we have somehow gotten away with it, and nothing sums up the moment more than the final text of the night that I send out to the three lads all at once. 'I love it when a plan comes together.'

The real bit of skill comes when we arrange everything. The ladies do not have to raise a finger. We keep telling them that all they have to do is think about where they want to shop and what they want to eat. Rhys has already sorted out the four tickets for the match, so all he has to do is work out how we get from the hotel to the stadium and then back again. His work here is almost complete.

I take charge of the hotel. I'm more than aware that this is the one mistake that could ruin everything. If the shower isn't sparkling, if there are cockroaches crawling, if the sheets are stiff then the mission will be a failure. As one we agree it is worth going a little bit further up market than we would have gone if it was only the boys, but if a luxurious hotel prevents us being in trouble then it's worth it.

Dave sorts out the travel. After some debate

it's decided that taking the train is the best bet. No one wants to drive the day after a rugby international, and if we took either a couple of cars or a minibus, it was a sure-fire bet that we'd be asking one of the girls to drive home, thus all of the Brownie points earnt over the weekend would be lost and gone forever.

Finally, Rob has the role of female liaison officer. He's been with his partner the shortest amount of time and will therefore get away with 'checking in' more regularly than the rest of us. He will be trusted to feedback to us if we are overstepping the mark or if the girls aren't getting on. We all agree that his role is priceless.

I managed to fuck things up anyway of course.

The journey is a dream, and even the weather, as we step out of the station, favours us as the sky clears and the sun beams down, giving the winter afternoon a romantic edge. The hotel is walking distance and the stroll only heightens the fact that we are in the good books.

The girls are smiling, chatting, happy. We men are smug, almost too confident that we have all the bases covered. As if to emphasise our excellent endeavour to ensure that pre-planning prevents piss poor performance, Rob whispers that the ladies would love a coffee. We pause at the next Starbucks, deposit our loved ones at a table and offer to go on ahead with the bags to check in. They swoon and I swear we could all smell the knicker elastic melting right there and then. As we swipe credit cards at the hotel we feel like we've already won the following day's rugby match, somehow, magically, each of us scoring the decisive try in the last move of the match.

"Any idea what the girls want for dinner tonight?" Dave asks.

"Chinese," Rob replies. There's no gap between question and answer.

I ask the hotel concierge which is the best Chinese restaurant in town. I ask him to book a table and we're set for an eight o'clock sit down.

"And can you have a taxi pick us up at seven?" Dave the transport asks. "And also book us one for noon tomorrow, destination Murrayfield!"

We all cheer. The concierge confirms the details and we're set to go.

"Quick beer to celebrate our success?" I suggest.

"Girls won't be happy. Coffee and afternoon sex all round," Rob reels off, robotic, Terminator stylie. None of us are complaining. He's taken to his job with gusto. We cannot fail. Despite being men, we believe we cannot fail.

Let's just say that we went back to meet our lovely ladies and the rest of the afternoon went with a bang.

Rosie and I come down from our room at ten to seven, just as the rest of the girls are heading down too.

"Thought you'd have been in the bar with the rest of them," says Di, Rhys's fiancée.

"No, no," I smile. "We were chatting while Rosie got ready." Now fair play, Rosie beams with the same smugness I had been feeling since we got on the train.

"Dave was the same," his wife, Jackie said. "But he was doing my head in so I sent him to get a drink."

Inwardly I cursed Dave. If he riled one of them up it was possible they could all get snippy.

"I'm loving all the attention," Julie said, Rob's girlfriend. At least the female liaison officer could be relied on to nail it. "But even Rob's not being as good as you!"

I grin. Maybe I'd missed out on my vocation for this trip after all!

My heart sinks when I see the three lads in the bar and six empty pint pots. "Jesus, guys," I whisper. "How fast are you sinking them? Tomorrow is the big one!"

"Rob was showing us a drinking game. It's class," Rhys said. "What's it called again?"

"Cardinal Puff," Rob said. "You have to remember a bunch of actions and down your pint in three."

"Tomorrow!" I implore, and the lads nod as the concierge comes over to tell us our taxis are ready. Rosie is proper delighted and she squeezes my hand as we leave the hotel.

"This weekend was a great idea," she says.

I wonder why we ever left the room.

The winning streak keeps on rolling. The restaurant is top notch. Because it's a Friday night it's an all-you-can-eat buffet, but the standard of food is great. The girls share a couple of bottles of wine and the lads listen about taking it steady on the ale, and we just have a couple of bottles of beer each. The girls make it clear that our good behaviour has been noted and not one of them makes a comment about how we are all going to be getting some later.

As the meal starts to come to a close, the ladies suggest going on to the pub opposite the restaurant. It doesn't look especially loud or busy but we ain't going to complain. The girls still have half a bottle of wine left, and they all want dessert, so they encourage us to go on ahead and get a table!"

We settle the bill as we leave, and as soon as we're in the pub we're high fiving each other. Nothing could make this go any better. Unfortunately, as I was shortly to find out, there was plenty to make it go wrong.

"Four pints," Rhys says to the barman, pointing at the lager tap. "Cheers, mate, keep the change."

"I think our man here needs to meet Cardinal Puff," Dave says.

"I think so," Rob agrees as we take out seats at an oversized table. The place is half full and has a little wooden dance floor by the door. We're sat so the girls will see us across the floor when they come in. "Okay, this is what you do," Rob continues and puts his pint down in front of him.

I shake my head. I am not getting involved in this.

"I drink to the Cardinal Puff for the first time," he says, lifts his glass and tilts it in a small salute. He puts the pint down and extends one finger of each hand. He taps the tops of the table once, the bottom of the table once, the front of his thighs once, the back of his thighs once and then stands up and sits down. He picks up his pint and downs about half of it. He repeats the process but starts off with, "I drink to the Cardinal Puff for the second time," only this time he does all of the actions twice, leaves just a small amount of beer in his glass and then goes through it a third time, with three sets of actions and finally finishes his drink.

I want to try. Simple as that. It's now a competition. It's a competition I need to take part in just to draw level. I stand up and look out of the front window of the pub and over the road. The girls are just getting ready to leave the restaurant.

I've got one shot at this!

I sit down again and nod at my mates, a look of determination etched across my face. "I drink to the Cardinal Puff for the first time," I begin, and so starts my descent into Hell.

The drinking and the routine to please the Cardinal Puff become autonomous. My mind is focussed on two things. The speed that the girls can get across the road and the rumbling sensation in my belly. My belly, chock full of Chinese buffet. The gassy beer is the catalyst that starts an unholy chemical reaction, and as the last dregs of the golden liquid slide down my throat because I am a man and I cannot give up when victory is so damn close, and the lads are cheering me on, but I know I've gone to far, and now there's no way to go back.

I'm going to puke.

I stand up. I look left, I look right.

I'm going to puke.

I can't see any signs for the toilets. I hop from one foot to the next.

I'm going to puke.

I have to rush out into the street. It's the only choice I have. I can feel a massive burp building up at the base of my throat, and I know that the belch is going to be more than gas. It is going to be a vile conglomerate of lager and oriental cuisine. Crispy duck with body temperature beer. Spring rolls that were once crispy but that are now soft and squidgy. Rice, noodles, chicken, all balled up in a carbonated ball, ready to explode.

I'm going to puke. Now!

I take a step towards the door just as it begins to open and I'm met face to face with our four girls, and they are all looking so happy, so relaxed, so pretty, and at first those smiles don't fade as I initially rush towards them and then pivot on my heels, turning back into the pub, realising that my escape route is blocked and that I need to find the toilet and then it happens.

Projectile is not the word. The Exorcist had less

expulsion to deal with. Even if I had an old priest and a young priest with all of the Holy water in the world trying to compel me right there, right then, there was still no hope of my soul being saved.

Puke exploded out of my mouth, and I saw the detail in a moment. It was thick, gloopy and yet fluid. It was viscous but lumpy. It stank of food, of beer, of sick. It gushed out of both of my nostrils at once, and I felt my face become hot and constricted. The splash as it hit the wooden dance floor, for some reason, reminded me of sand thrown up on a long jumper's landing.

And then I made it worse by jamming my hand over my mouth. The next surge of vomit simply leaked down over my shirt, onto my trousers, over my shoes. I could hear the girls gagging, the lads retching, and the bar man screaming for me to get the fuck out. I stumbled though the girls, each of them mimicking me with their hands up over their mouths, and out of the door. The cold fresh air cleared my head and stomach almost immediately, but I shoved my head into a nearby rubbish bin just in case. The smell of puke on my clothes hit me again and I vommed a final gut full into the black plastic bin liner.

"Oh, shit. Oh, shit. Oh, shit." I gasped. In

retrospect I was lucky there weren't any police about. I was in enough trouble as it was."

Now our Geezer will be the first to admit that he deserved everything he got that night in Edinburgh. Despite making every effort, above and beyond the call of duty, he still let himself down by slipping into 'lad' mode for just five minutes in an otherwise elegant performance. Was it truly our hero's fault though? Should his best friends not take some responsibility? The answer to that lies with the girls. If you were our Geezer's lovely Rosie, who would you blame? And if you were one of the other lad's partners? Blame is a transient beast. At the end of the day, and the end of his lads' weekends away forever, it is our so-nearly-the-hero who is the only one who actually has to live with the fallout. Each and every time he fancies a beer. Each and every time he says he's going out with his mates. And even when the poor bugger has food poisoning or the 'flu. You can hear it now, can't you?

"That's nowhere near as sick as you got in that pub in Edinburgh."

Echoing. Forever.

It's (not) a Thriller!

Men and women can be distinguished by many things. Their taste in clothing. Their preferred food. The amount of time they spend in the bathroom. Their ability to quote random sporting trivia at will. Their genitalia. There are more subtle differences. Like women preferring love-laden Hugh Grant or Colin Firth movies while men choose the torture horror of someone having to hack their own foot off to live. Women slide the new Sophie Kinsella off the bookshelf while men extol the virtues of a good Stephen King. Now, there's no problem here, is there? Is there?

Well, there shouldn't be because, let's face it, most women don't really expect their man, no matter how much they dream of him being sickeningly romantic, to memorise the proposal speech from Pride and Prejudice. No matter what they watch or read, our girls are, if nothing else, realistic. And men, no matter how much they think it would be great to smash through a bathroom door with an axe and scream 'Here's Jonny,' they'd never do it. They would not want to scare their partners. Or would they?

Sometimes of course it *can* be a man's choice of fiction that can become his novel yet unintentional way of attracting trouble. He may simply be trying to illustrate that he is more than a rugby-loving, brain-dead lump of meat by sharing his love of literature. How is he to know that it can backfire, and backfire very, very badly?

Alex, 34, Food Technician, Barnsley.

"I'd been dating Mikey for about a month when I took him out to meet a few of my work friends. He was a bit nervous because, I guess, I'd built my friends up a bit as a bunch of brains because they are all scientists in some shape or form. Mikey's got a good job but he looks a bit...ummm... Mikey spends a lot of the time in the gym. He...doesn't look like a scientist...ummm... I was a bit worried too. So I stuck to him like glue for most of the evening, but then I had to go to the loo, and on the way back, one of the girls stops me for a catch up, and I see Connie start a conversation with a terrified looking Mikey. I try to free myself but it takes too long, and by the time I get over there and try to rescue him, I see he's doing alright...ummm...he surprised me.

"He's talking about books with her.

"I was blown away. He was trying so hard. Anyway, the rest of the night goes really well and the following Monday I'm about to leave for work when Mikey stops me at the door, runs back up the stairs to his bedroom, and comes back down with a book. 'Give this to Connie,' he says and goes on to tell me it's his favourite book and that she'd said it was a book she'd always wanted to read but had never got around to it. I'm thinking he's even more fantastic than I thought. A few days later, Connie appears at my desk and virtually throws the book down. 'If that's his favourite book, I'd sleep with one eye open, if I were you,' she tells me.

"I'm shocked...ummm...I didn't know what to say...ummm. I hadn't even looked to see what the book was.

"'Seriously,' she continues,' If you don't believe me, turn to page three hundred and fifty.'

"I do as she asks, and in the book the narrator is describing how he's eating his girlfriend's intestines! I close the book and turn to the front cover. It's 'American Psycho' by Bret Easton Ellis. Look, I know I should have checked what kind of book it was, but I was in a rush, and he was making a real effort, and I was so proud of him...ummm...I just didn't realise he was going to lend horror porn to my workmates... Ummm...but come on? Who would? I don't take him to work events any more!"

It may be considered that it is not so much a man's preference for drawing inspiration from his favourite horror novel or movie that can get him in trouble, but rather their timing for when this passion manifests itself. A bit like breaking wind or peeing with the bathroom door wide open on the first date, freaking out our female counterparts at the start of a relationship does not bode well for future dalliances. While a man may think it is simply a bit of fun, a woman is more likely to wonder what they are letting themselves in for, in the longer term, and even what their new beau's true intentions for them are. It's one thing for a girl to think all the boy wants to do is get them into bed. It's another that they are scared they are going to become the next part of a biology dissection project.

Carrie, 27, Television Producer, Slough.

"Nigel and I had been set up by a mutual friend. I wasn't really up for it to start with, but she kept on and on about him, and in the end, I agreed to go for a drink one night. He was pretty cool. Funny. Courteous. I'd go as far to say gentlemanly. We met for drinks the following week, and then went out for dinner. There was no way he was letting me pay, and I knew, just knew, that he didn't expect anything on the back of it. I also got the feeling that I wouldn't be able to return the favour, that he'd always want to pay. He just came across as one of those genuinely nice guys, so instead of suggesting we dine out for our next date, I invited him around to my place for dinner. He agreed as long as he could bring the wine and dessert. Like I said, he was being a proper gent. I liked him. He wasn't arrogant or smug. He wasn't too into fashion or the gym or anything, he was just normal. Or so I thought! Anyway, he arrives smack on time and I'm still preparing the food and he joins me in the kitchen, pours me a glass of wine, and asks if he can help. I set him to chopping some veggies and we're in my little kitchen, stood back to back, chatting away. I remember feeling really at ease with him and I tell him so. I remember exactly what I said. 'I must trust you, inviting you back here so early. For all I know you could be some sort of serial killer.' And he makes no response so I turn around and he's stood there with this *mental* look on his face, his eyes all wide, staring right at me. And he's got the biggest knife in the kitchen held up level with his face, and then he *grins*! I'm not sure if that was meant to diffuse his misplaced humour, but it made him look like a psycho. I nearly ran out of my own place! I gave him a right telling off, but I still don't think he got how un-funny it was. We're still together. Things are great, really, really great, and I think he knows how close he came to blowing it that night. As far as I can tell, he's not told a soul."

It doesn't take first-night nerves to make a mountain out of a molehill when it comes to the man behaving in a way that scares his lady. In fact, it can be the familiarity and comfort of routine that can present a husband with a gold-plated opportunity to scare his wife witless. As far as the ladies are concerned though, it is these well thought-out and planned misdemeanours that rile them the most. It's one thing to quickly duck behind the sofa and leap out, but it's another to plot and plan some Halloween-style japery that Michael Myers, Jason Vorhees and Freddie Kruger would be proud of. As Clive found out to his peril.

Clive, 31, Computer Engineer, Ilfracombe.

"We live in a third floor apartment, and Ros hates the fact that I smoke. She won't even just let me smoke out of the window. I have to go all the way down to the main entrance on the ground floor and smoke outside. Obviously, every time I fancy a cigarette, it rains. I realised early on that this was all part of her plan to get me to quit. She knew I'd have to go outside to smoke if we went out and that I hated it, so she was employing the same theory at home. Now, I have to concede that it was starting to work. She wouldn't pause anything we were watching if I wanted to go outside, she wouldn't delay food being ready. Look, it caused a few rows, but I did understand that she was trying to get me to quit as much for me as for her. It's not like she was actually being selfish. That didn't stop me from getting a bit annoyed though. Anyway, one evening we've been watching one of those movie clip programmes. You know the ones. It was something like the 100 greatest movies, or actors or something, and the Norman Bates shower scene was in there. Ros says how much she always got upset by Hitchcock films because it was the implied threat that was more disturbing to her than the outright gore of a full-on slasher movie. So I sit there for a few minutes and my mind is whirring and I'm sure I'm grinning like an idiot, but once I've got it right in my mind I stand up and say I'm going outside for a cigarette. I make a big deal of shouting bye when I'm at the front door and make sure it closes pretty loudly so she can hear it."

A deep sigh tells us that Ros certainly *did* hear the door close as Clive had intended. Clive raises his eyebrows but just about manages to suppress the smile that is threatening to agitate Ros even further. To be fair, with a nod and a motion of his hand he offers her the chance to give a different side of the story.

Ros, 29, Landscape Designer, Ilfracombe.

"Yeah, I heard it all right. Like I heard it on the hour, every hour for the whole time we lived there. I *hated* him smoking. *Hated it*! It just disrupted everything. But that's not what you want to hear, is it? Okay, so he's gone out for a smoke and I potter about for a minute or two. I put the kettle on, I put away a few pots and pans, and then I decide to go to the loo. I turn the light on, close the door, and I start, well, *going*. And then the shower curtain flies open and that numpty screams out at the top of his voice! I nearly fell off the toilet. My heart is pounding like it never had before, and although I've quickly realised it's only Clive and not some mass murderer, I can't help it and I start to cry. Not a few tears either, but full on sobs. I guess there was still a little tiny bit inside of me that thought I was about to get killed while my man, my protector was outside puffing away on his disgusting habit. And all he can do is stand there, in the shower, killing himself laughing. I swear to God I wished he'd do himself an injury, like a hernia or something. When I pulled myself together I turned the shower on and soaked him, but it made no difference. He just doubled up even more. And look at him? Laughing about it again now. But who had the last laugh? Come on, Clive, tell them! Clive? Tell them how long you went without sex? Go on! Or maybe how long it's been since you last smoked? He might not be saying but I'll tell you straight, as funny as he found it, I've enjoyed my revenge more."

But of course no man could be so stupid as to shoot himself in the foot once he has convinced his loved one to put aside her fears and watch a much anticipated horror movie with him, would they? Let's face it boys, it doesn't kill us to partake of the occasional chick flick, does it? Katie Hudson, Anne Hathaway or Julia Roberts in yet another wedding dress are not exactly going to induce night terrors. Even Patrick Swayze saying 'Nobody puts Baby in a corner,' before sashaying into the camera, flicking his dodgy eighties mullet from side to side, will have us double checking under the bed to make sure the bogeyman isn't there, will he? Well, not after the first time, anyway. So when we have been able to talk, coerce or bribe our girlfriends or wives to sit for an hour and a half to watch something they would not choose to see in a million years, it is our duty not to screw it up. Isn't it?

Darren, 38, History Teacher, York.

"Mandy doesn't really enjoy films, full stop. She finds the cinema a little claustrophobic so we tend not to go. I'd like to go now and again but I catch up on DVD at home. She'll do something else if I really want to watch a film, like reading or just pottering around the house. This one evening she was tired and I was flicking through the TV channels and saw that 'Paranormal Activity' was on Pay Per View. She wasn't too enamoured with the little description they give you, but I had an older film magazine that raved about it and I managed to convince her to give it a go. So just before it starts she put on her PJs and slippers and makes herself really cosy on the sofa. I get what she's doing without making a big deal about it. She's making sure she's not got to move for the duration, so she can not have to think what's hiding out in the hall. She's being pretty cool about it, and I make sure she knows I'm really pleased and owe her plenty. The movie starts and it's as good as everyone had said. I'm loving it, and to my, and I guess her, surprise, so is she. Well, I wouldn't say Mandy's enjoying it as such but she's not walked out and she's looking totally engrossed in it. I think it helped that we *both* jumped at the same bits. See that's the thing about a really good scary movie. Even if you've seen all the other scary movies, a good one scares you in ways that you are least expecting. Now, she did watch the last fifteen minutes through her fingers, like I'd have watched Doctor Who as a kid, but when it ended, she turned to me and said something like it was better than she thought. Not that she'd never watch anything like it again, or that I was sick for liking such things, but that she'd maybe consider going to see the sequel, which was due out. Now, I'm delighted with this, which makes what I did next all the more stupid. Mandy gets up and goes to the loo. And then I react with no thought of the consequences. I'm up on my feet, I sprint to the kitchen and straight to that over-stuffed draw of junk that everyone has in their kitchen. I pull out a spool of black thread and snap off a length. I run back to the lounge and tie one end of the cotton to one of Mandy's slippers. I trail the cotton around the leg of the television stand and then down the side of my chair. I hear the flush of the loo just as I sit down, cotton in hand. Mandy sits down and wants to talk about the film, about horror movies in general, and as we chat, every now and then I reel in a little more cotton until her slipper moves a solitary inch. She doesn't notice. I do it again, this time a little bit more and this time she does see it and she lets out this little yelp that she cuts off halfway through, and then she gives me a look that was scarier than anything that happened in the film. Spare room for three nights, publicly derided and never allowed to choose a movie again. In retrospect, I think I got away lightly."

So when it comes to mimicking the scary monsters and super creeps of the realms of fantasy and horror, men are advised to leave it to the professionals. Having spent any amount of effort to have won our way, even for the smallest of things such as choosing the genre of movie, the last thing we should be thinking of doing is throwing away this concession. Yet we do. Consistently. Constantly. Calamitously. And the worse thing is that we'd probably do it again.

Let's Get Physical, Physical!

From a very early age, men are obsessed with women's bodies. This allegedly soon becomes body part specific and men openly categorise themselves as predominant fans of either 'boobs' or 'bums'. This in itself is not likely to earn them rapturous rounds of applause from the female of the species. Why would it? Throughout history, women have had to battle for their rights. From being given the vote, to membership in the armed forces and to being inspirational captains of industry, women have proven time and time again that they are the equal of men, and in fact, our betters in numerous arenas, and still for most men on the street it all comes down to the 'rack' or the 'booty'.

Is this fair? Of course it's not! If a woman was to behave in this way, of judging men by their looks, they'd be classed as shallow and, most likely, a slut. Also, most men would never get any! But when the most popular man in the pub describes women in this way, then they are the confident Jack the Lad that everyone else wishes they could be like. Let's be honest, such conversations happen. That is a fact. When they happen between a group of like-minded men, this type of chit-chat is harmless enough and can cause no offence. It may be said that such behaviour is an outlet which should allow men to vent their attitudes among like-minded (insert word of choice here) without incurring the wrath of any women. If only that were actually the case. Whereas women may subtly suggest that Johnny Depp is an interesting and talented actor who they would love to get to know, men are unlikely to utilise such terms. Instead, a very literal head to toe description would ensue. From legs that stretch all the way up to the arse to lips that look capable of performing magical tricks, a man can provide a map of a woman while bypassing the personality. A description said out loud, in front of the person they are describing, in an attempt to draw or maintain their interest, men think it will actually work. Because physically 'complimentary' chat up lines always work, don't they?

Leanne, 31, Business Manager, Eastbourne.

"Look, I don't find meeting guys easy. It goes with the job. I take my career seriously, and because of that, I don't have that much time to go out meeting people, so when I do, I end up being really picky. It's not difficult to remain true to my standards though. Have you seen what's out there? No, let me restate that. Have you *heard* what's out there? The thing is that I'm successful. I'm educated. I've got more letters after my name than I've got in my name. But no one I meet, no one I talk to, asks about that. They can't see past the size of my chest. It's always been a problem. I was the first girl in school to get them and they arrived with a bang. I'll never get used to men's obsession with them. And I'll never get past the ridiculous way in which men think that opening a conversation with me with a reference to my bra size will make me want to down my drink and drag them home to bed. Seriously, I've heard it all. The most often used one? 'I bet you don't get many of those to the pound?' Classy, eh? The type of idiot that says that to me probably doesn't even know how many ounces there are in a pound, let alone anything else. One guys asked me if he could move into my bra. Another one said he was a scaffold engineer and would I like to be checked for Health and Safety. I've had a bloke walk up to me and pretend he'd been poked in the eye, I'm assuming by my breast, and then ask me if I wanted to buy him a drink to make up for the injury! Oh my God! Another guy, and I really thought this one was being a gentleman, walked up to me in a bar and asked could he hang my coat up for me. For a moment I was impressed. He took my coat and then tried to hang it up off *me*! Off my *front*! When it fell to the floor he asked if he could hang it off the back of his chair and would I like to join him. I turned around and walked out. The number of men who can't even look me in the face is ridiculous. I know it's a cliché but I really do have to say 'my face is eight inches north of there' on a weekly basis. If it happened in work I'd be firing people left right and centre. God, I'm getting angry just thinking about this. How can men even think this kind of approach is going to work? You know what the worst attempt was? I was being shown to my table at a very exclusive restaurant, joining colleagues from a rival business, when a man in a suit at the adjacent table sees me coming and announces to his cohort, 'Whoa! Dead heat in a Zeppelin race!'

His table explodes in laughter and I'm humiliated. I take my seat, trying to regain some professional respect, but I'm unable to see beyond the smirks, and then he sends me over a glass of champagne. Not as an apology but as an attempt to get my phone number. Look, if this is the way forward in the singles' market then the human race is in a mess. Why can't men see beyond my breasts? And if they can't? Then they should learn to keep their damn mouths shut!"

But despite men's lack of social skills, we still, obviously more by luck than by judgement, manage to find ourselves a partner. I'm surprised that thousands of men aren't sat there with a look of complete shock on their faces, even as they sit and hold hands with a loved one over the restaurant table, wondering how they found themselves in such a pleasant position. However, it does not take us long to screw things up. It could be weeks, months or even years before we reach that point where complacently kicks in and we make a stupid comment or refer to a body part in a derogatory manner, but it will happen. Of course it will. We're men. We're useless. And all it can take is the smallest trigger. A comment that we manage to turn on its head and make something negative out of something that should have been so, so positive.

Emma, 27, Personnel Officer, Wrexham.

"Stu and I got married after being together for about two years. From word go, he was very complimentary about my rear. Not in a cheesy or laddish way, but it was definitely his favourite of my features. Even in his wedding speech he made reference to how much he loved, and I quote, 'my perfect little bum'. I'm not saying he was obsessed with it, and it wasn't something he'd say in public. It was our little thing and I liked it. I need to put this across properly to be fair to him. It's not like he'd pat me on the butt in front of all of his mates or grope it when he popped into work to see me. It was, like I said, our little thing. What I didn't realise was just how important the word 'little' was to Stu. We had a joint gym membership, and while I was pleased that neither of us was over the top with it, we managed to go together pretty regularly. It was good fun but after a few months I got a promotion in work, and I just didn't have the time to go anymore. Well, not as often as we used to and therefore not as often as Stu. I kind of suggested that I might give up my membership and he kind of suggested that I should consider the impact of putting on a little bit of weight. I asked him what he'd say or do if I did put on a few pounds. He shook his head and said he wasn't quibbling over a couple of pounds. Then he pauses, looks me right in the eye, and with a smile says, 'But if you put on half a stone, I think I'd have to have a quiet word with you.' I was gob-struck. *Have a word!* Can you imagine how confused I was? How insulted I was? What would that word be? Goodbye? Fatty? Exercise? I don't know what I expected that word to be specifically, but I knew it wasn't going to be a good one. So I ask him what he expects to happen when we have a baby. Apparently that's different. Do you reckon it's different that he's not quit the gym too? And that he had a six pack when we first met and now? Rotund is not the word for it, so, well, let's just say that maybe I need to be having a word with him these days!"

Women are of course not as superficial as men.

If the true love of their life were to add a few 'comfort' pounds, then a woman would hardly make a sound about it. In fact, they would see it as a sign that they were successfully ensuring that their man felt loved, appreciated and safe in their relationship. From a man's point of view, this is of course an incredibly annoying trait. What makes this acceptance of male failings all the more difficult to swallow is that if we try to reciprocate the sentiments then we are immediately classed as liars and being 'full of it'. We as men resent this. How women are able to sniff out our bullshit so quickly is beyond our comprehension. But they do, time and time again, which is why we can so easily get ourselves into trouble. And just because our widening waist bands are something tolerable and not worth making a silly comment about, then that does not mean that going from six pack to barrel is a painless experience. Obviously it could be, but we, as mortal men, find a way to draw attention to it in a manner that simply cannot be ignored. Why do we do this? Why do we do anything that is remotely risky? Because we can! Because we open our mouths and the words are out before the thought has fully formed inside our tiny little minds. There may be a precise point of no return that sings out at us as we fling ourselves towards it, but we choose to ignore it. For we are men, and men do not know what is best for them. Like shutting up. Or not opening our mouths in the first place.

Barry, 34, New Dad, Hull.

"It's always the little things that get you in the shit, isn't it? That one thing you say that is just a passing comment, not meaning to mean anything by it, and that's the thing they grab hold of. Of course it is. It's like they've been waiting and waiting and waiting to pick you up on something, and I'll tell you what, once it comes along? You're shafted! Pure and simple. Because they will not let it go, will they? Not in a million years. And I'll tell you what else they do. They save it up, don't they? They'll not mention it for a few weeks, the super-bad thing you've done wrong, but then, just when you think they've left it, no, out it comes again, and well, I'm sure you know the rest. The reason for my bitterness? Ridiculous. Ridiculous. The only word it deserves. Now since the baby was born I've got to give, and openly have given, loads of credit to the wife. I don't know how she does it. Katie's fulltime looking after the kiddie and she's still managed to lose all the baby weight. I'm not saying she's in the gym every day but she walks everywhere, and fair play, she may be tired all the time but she looks fantastic. And you know what? I've been telling Katie this loads, which makes this blow-up all the more stupid. Especially because I'm the one not doing the exercise. Look, I work fulltime and when I get in, I just want to be at home, with my *family*, you get it? So I know I've put on a bit of weight. Okay, a lot of weight, but I'll lose it again once we get into a set routine. The thing that got me in trouble was just a joke, a throwaway comment to her friend who came over to see the baby. I started off making a serious point and then realised maybe I was being a bit heavy, a bit too personal maybe. I said something like, *'It's really getting to me to see how quickly our little one is growing up. She understands words already and when I say some words she points to what they are and the majority of time correctly too. Simple stuff, like plate or cat, you know? It's just amazing. And she's getting more sophisticated with what words she's picking up on all the time too. For example, I said to her the other day, "Boobies" and she tried to pull her mother's top down. This was a happier ending than it could have been. She could have easily pointed at mine!'* Now come on? What's wrong with that? It was just a bit of fun. If anything I was highlighting how Katie had lost the weight while I'd put it on."

Barry's wife, Katie, has a clear understanding of what was wrong with Barry's behaviour and it has nothing to do with what he said. It was more to do with what he *did* as he said it, not that he has any recall of his failings in this department.

Katie, 30, New Mum, Hull.

"And that's it, is it? You said that, got a giggle and moved on? I wish I'd filmed it because I'd have put it on Youtube. You'd have been a global video phenomena, you pratt! You want to know what he *actually* did? I'll tell you. Yes, he said exactly what he's just quoted himself as saying. Word for word. I get what he was trying to do, and I'd not even thought up to that point that he felt the need to reassure me about any post-baby weight I was carrying, but clearly he did. Even that I can get over. No, what I can't get my head around is that, as he mentioned his own flourishing man boobs, he grabs hold of them and actually *jiggles* them around! It was like watching that fat kid from The Goonies doing the bloody Truffle Shuffle! For heaven's sake! He carried on wobbling around even after he stopped shaking himself. No one thought it was funny. He may think different but the laughs were just nervous reactions. He made himself, and me, look like fools! Now, when I play that game with the baby, when I say a name of something and wait for her to point, I've taught her a new word. Twit! She's gotten really good at it, too, because she points at him every single time!"

Of course, some people are able to put up with their husband's floppy physique, safe in the knowledge that he would never dream of making any reference to such sensitive issues. Maybe not raising expectations from day one is the way forward to a long and happy marriage. That and knowing when to keep our mouths shut.

Gloria, 68, Retired, Swansea.

"Now, what's the point in me worrying about that? He's always loved his food and he's always loved his pint, so he's had a belly ever since I've known him. Even when he was young, like. I don't see the problem with it. It makes him more cuddly, and I loves a good cuddle, I does. And what's this about: *has he ever criticised my body*? He might look daft but he's not stupid now, is he? Bloody hell, he might pay attention to the telly a bit more if that girl in the swimsuit from that Sean Connery film is on, but then, I sit up a bit when Sean's on there too, so what's the harm?"

The sentiment here is of course refreshing and for want of sounding mushy, simply lovely. But underneath the enduring love there is still the issue that eyes will wander. It may be Sean Connery and Ursula Andress. It could be Posh or Becks. Orlando Bloom or Keira Knightley. The list is endless, the combinations beyond the comprehension of even the greatest mathematic minds. It is one thing to look. Men and women alike are guilty, in the least offensive definition of the word. You may even have your 'top five' on a laminated list like Ross from Friends. That's all well and good, and unless one of you becomes a stalker, it's pretty healthy. What will inevitably get a man in trouble is if his wandering eye is too obvious in other situations, like during a romantic dinner, or in the pub, down the gym or when shopping. Certain rules of etiquette should always be obeyed in these situations. Focus on your partner. Eyes down. Always. And even if you are out with the lads and do see something that you weren't expecting to see, don't go home and tell the wife. Please.

Dean, 28, Sales Advisor, Preston.

"First up, I want to be clear that just because I am saying that this is about 'a mate' I'm not using code for it actually being about me. I've got enough stories to tell you when I've screwed up, big time, but I'm positive you'd have heard them, or something similar before. What my mate, Don, did on my stag do is something special. No one else would have got himself hung, drawn and quartered the way he did. I ain't gonna waste your time with me pissing on the side of the wardrobe when I've got this little beauty up my sleeve. Will you print his real name? Surname too? That doesn't matter because I'm gonna make sure *everyone* knows it's him anyway! It's my stag do and we went to Liverpool for the night. Got to say it was brilliant. Liverpool is one of those places that just lends itself to a good party. The atmosphere was cracking and we even had our photos taken with some footballers. It was well cool. So the night goes on and before we know it we're down to a hard core of about six of us, the ones who are sharing a minibus back home. Me, my two brothers, my future brother-in-law, another mate, and Don. Surprisingly, it's the brother-in-law who suggests we end the night at a titty bar, a strip club, you know. What can I say? We're gonna be family, so I don't want to fall out with him, so off we go. Funnily enough, he knows just where to go, and we walk into a place that is crawling with topless totty. We all try to be cool as we walk over to a table, sit down and order some drinks, and then we turn around and see Don is still stood in the door, his mouth open, his tongue almost hanging out, and his eyes wide like someone's jumped out and given him a fright. We finally get him to sit at the table, but the look on his face hasn't changed. 'I've never been in one of these places before,' he whispers to me, and of course, I make him repeat it out loud for everyone to hear. I think a couple of people laughed, but most were just glad he hadn't had a stroke. A medical stroke, I mean, not a *stroke* stroke! So we have a couple of beers, and I can see the lads collecting money together, and I know they're gonna pay for a lap dance for me. I get this light bulb moment when I know it could be loads better, so I lean over and suggest to my brother that it might be much more fun if Don got the lap dance. Well, word flies around the table and we're all in agreement so we set it up. Jesus, the moronic look on his face as she led him away to a private booth! Forrest Gump had nothing on him. We can't resist so we peak around the corner and he's just sat there, respectful almost, with his hands on his knees, and that look, *that grin*, plastered across his face. And then, to cap it all, when the dance finishes and she's trying to pull her miniscule clothes back on, he leans in and gives her a hug! He hugged his lap dancer! Well, I thought I'd seen it all! I hadn't. The minibus picks us up and he's like a puppy dog, a puppy dog that's in a dreamland. We get back to Preston, and he's staying at my house and his wife is staying there too. Now when we get in, the two girls get up. Not to check if we'd been good, just for the crack like, to have a laugh and I think to check if the boys had shaved my head. 'How was your night, boys?' his wife asks. 'I had a lovely girl dance for me,' Don says, and before I can shut him up he continues, 'A real lovely girl. I don't not what she's doing working there, though.' I can't help him now. 'Working where?' his wife asks, the tone getting cold. 'The strip club! But I gave her a hug and told her she should go back to college and...' She grabs him by the ear, seriously, right by the earlobe and drags him up the stairs. Me and my wife had to go into the back garden so they couldn't hear us laughing. Seriously, it was one thing giving her a bloody hug, but telling his wife? Are you sure you can't print surnames? Or addresses?"

So maybe we can keep our mouths shut and not make less than flattering comments about our lady's ever expanding everything. For once, we button it and forego emphasising our own burgeoning, bouncing breasts. Maybe, just maybe, we simply do not draw attention to the fact that we have never shown any inclination in having a fine physique. Maybe we learn that our loved one is not as shallow as us, that they are happy with us they way we are. Did you hear that? I said they're actually happy! With us! Wow! Picture that. Bliss all round. For once, we've not have got it all wrong. And then we say something daft, something that had no right being said, like, oh, let me think, that we gave a stripper a hug, and surprise, surprise, our world collapses around our ears. And yet we never learn, do we?

And if we haven't learned how to behave by the time we are, say, thirty (okay, for the lads, let's say forty) then imagine what a man's attitude to the human body was like when he was but a teenager. And we're not talking about a teenage boy's attitude towards anyone else's body because at that age, it would seem, he doesn't even have any respect for his own. And of course, when a teenage boy gets it wrong, it's not a girlfriend he has to worry about pissing off. When you're fourteen it's much worse, because the one only woman you can piss off is your mum. And you really don't want to do that because she'll remember forever. And tell everyone.

Terry, 45, Colorado, Advertising Executive.
"I had my first experience of 'self love' when I was fourteen. I didn't go near it again

for nearly a year afterwards. What happened? What went wrong? Everything, that's what. I'm not going into detail of the actual act itself but suffice to say it was me, my penis, my right hand and a ripped out page of a porn mag. Job done, I listened carefully at my bedroom door, making sure that the television downstairs was still on a show and not on the commercials. Yep, Cagney and Lacey were still trying to solve a crime, so I scuttled across to the bathroom, wearing nothing but my t-shirt. I heard a noise from my brother's room. My younger brother's room. My brother who could often annoy the Hell out of me, so I decided I'd rub my first step into manhood in his face. I tapped on his door, opened it a crack and whispered what I'd been up to and that I was now the man of the house. I closed the door behind me and entered the bathroom, and I know now that I was distracted because I'd not got a response off of him. Anyway, I cleaned my 'deposit' up and then realised that I could see 'it' in the mirror, dangling nicely under the bottom of my t-shirt. So I start dancing, admiring my manly form as it jigged up and down, lifting my t-shirt with it. I was a

Goddamn love machine. I was the man! And then my mum's voice stopped me in my tracks. 'What do you think you are doing to yourself?' she shouted. I hadn't closed the bathroom door properly and it had swung open. I'm not sure how long she'd been stood there, but she must have seen plenty. And the tissues from my clean-up mission were still on display too. I panicked. 'Where's Dad?' I asked, feeling the need to discuss my action with another male, someone who would surely know not just what I'd been up to but more importantly why! I wish I hadn't asked. 'He's in talking to your brother about his exam results.' In talking to my brother! Who I had just detailed my first hand job experience to! The wonderful sensation of my intimate moment long forgotten, I promptly threw up into the sink, on top of my spunky tissues. Was that the worst of it? No. The worst of it was how many times the story got told. In school by my brother. Down the local pub by my Dad. And to every girl I ever brought home by my mum. Okay, yes, the job here was a great opportunity, but was it the real reason I left the UK? What the fuck do you think?"

Memoir of a Geezer

Men will lose whatever 'hotness' they may have had before their girlfriend or wife. Let's all agree that this is a fact. Please. Of course one of the many reasons why a man may lose his Adonis-like physique may be because of issues of a genetic nature, and therefore out of his control. It may be down to deep rooted psychological issues relating to self perception and body-confidence. Or, as our Geezer demonstrates, it may be due to becoming a greedy pig at a young age and not wanting to change the habits of a lifetime.

The Lunchbox Kid

"Now what do you do when you're eight years old and you've been ditched by your girlfriend for your best-friend, your best-friend no longer wants to be your friend anymore, your desk buddy tells the teacher on you for copying during the weekly spelling test, the teacher's pet laughs at you in front of your class for not knowing the eight-times table, and one of your friends calls dibs on your morning break treats, swigs most of your bubblegum flavoured Panda Pop, and steals the last of your Smarties?

I tell you what you do. You eat their lunch!

However I feel that I'm being somewhat dishonest here. As the aforementioned *reasons to why I ate my fellow classmates' lunches* is not an exhaustive list, I could and should also add the following;

- I had spent all my daily school dinner money at the corner shop on the way to school, mainly on Mars bars. The resultant affect being that by dinner time, I was hungrier than a rabid cannibal.
- I had lost that days dinner ticket (on the odd week when I actually spent my money on school dinner tickets), and was too scared of getting another telling-off from the dinner ticket collecting lady.
- Just because I was addicted to my classmates' sandwiches.

Now... I say sandwiches. Again this is not entirely true either. I was partial to a classmates' Penguin biscuit bar, a Trio or even a '5, 4, 3, 2, 1' wafer biscuit too. And I never stopped there. If there was half a bag of crisps left, then I had been known (only to myself of course) to tuck into those as well, especially if they were pickled onion Monster Munch, or any of the Marvel Superhero varieties.

So how did this come about you ask? To be honest I can't tell you. I can only assume it came out of hunger and for some of the reasons listed in the introductory paragraph. For whatever reason, that day I had no dinner money. It had nothing to do with the classroom tray marked with my name having five or six Mars bars hidden beneath my school books, by the way. I believe that hunger landed heavy in my belly and stimulated a hunter's reaction. The idea of thieving my classmates' lunches was surely justified in the early days as *'hey, dinnertime has been and gone, what is left is what they don't want, so that is okay to eat.'* The concept was perfectly justifiable, yet perfectly wrong, all at the same time. Nevertheless, my own self-justification merited this idea as one's natural survival instincts, and I was hungry. That made it okay. To me. And I was the only one I had to justify it to. So there!

So how did I go about the thieving you ask? This was easy, though the timing was key. Midway through the afternoon period, approximately thirty minutes after dinnertime was over, I'd raise my hand aloft and ask to be excused from class for a toilet break. Now, with some trial and error I found thirty minutes to be the most acceptable time to be dismissed from class without the *"Dinnertime has only just finished, why didn't you go during dinner?"* or the *"It is only x amount of time before the school bell rings* (marking the end of the schooling day), *you'll just have to wait,"* blurb from Mrs. Teacher. So on random days throughout the week, fortnight and month, I asked for a toilet recess approximately thirty minutes post dinner break, met as always (pardoning the initial trial and errors of course) with a nod of Mrs. Teacher's head, her mark of approval. I may have been eight, but I had strategy, and part of that was not to develop a trend that raised suspicion.

Once out of the classroom, deception was not an issue. I didn't have to sneak past the glass panels of the classroom door as I would have to when I got to ten years of age and wanted to sneak down to the sport hall to watch the girls do gym in those little knickers. No, the peach of this plan was that my class's cloakroom was an immediate right out of the classroom door and through a set of heavy fire exit doors, as were the boy's toilets. I feel I should offer you, the reader, an evil laugh at this point, however I think perhaps this is better served up later. The cloakroom itself was two box rooms immediately left and right off of the corridor leading to the upper school play-yard: girls to the left and boys to the right of the corridor. No coat pegs were assigned a name and it was just a free-for-all, and whatever peg was available when you got there, was your peg for that day. And this added a spice of excitement to the thievery. I never knew whose bag was whose, and therefore what delights I'd find within them. It was a lottery of doggy bags. All I had to do was rummage beneath the coats (*because beneath the coats, all bags are hidden and safe!*), unzip, unbuckle or depress the clasps on the bags, and I was literally in for a treat of sloppy seconds.

Timing, of course, was key. Within six to eight minutes I was sat back in my classroom next to the monkey man Mark Priest and big boobs Carol Bailey. Yes even at eight years of age, Carol Bailey's chest was far more bumpy when compared to the other females of the species in our class. And I loved them...it...her, um. No wonder I didn't notice naked dancer Rhian until my later teens! Now, timing was everything to my survival for that afternoon's period of class. Perhaps I should say *timings*? Yes, that's right, this single post-dinner break thief feast of the day churned an ugly desire for more feasting, and I quickly derived a craving for a morning get-me-by. Kiddies' elevenses if you please. The lure of fresh pre-dinner break sandwiches still wrapped up tight, the unspoilt circular foil on juice cartons, and even the unbitten pleasure of ripened fruit (both of which were new to the morning menu) made my mouth water like Pavlov's dog. Coupled to this the small admittance that my thievery now occurred practically every day and not with the randomness my strategy once detailed. I was more cunning to find ways to escape the classroom and hide beneath the coats of my fellow children, gobbling their lovingly prepared lunches like a Gremlin after midnight. *Evil laugh* with me, if you will!

If one of my classmates was not feeling well, I knew it was School Rules that the child had to be accompanied to the School Nurse by a fellow pupil. I quickly became that pupil. I would usher my unwell classmate to the Nurses Office whether they wanted to or not, and then sprint around the back of the school, through the staff car par, onto the upper school yard where access to my classrooms cloakroom was just a door away and always out of sight from Mrs. Teacher and my classmates. Though time was of the essence, I only had two to three minutes compared to the six to eight afforded to me during the post-dinner break toilet stop.

Mrs. Teacher's class register had to be taken

back to the School Administration Office for something I didn't know back then following registration period. I was the one who demonstrated the most willingness to take on that responsibility. The quickest route to the Administration Office was an immediate right out of the classroom, through the heavy fire exit doors, into my classrooms cloakroom for a small nibble, and then out onto the upper play-yard, down the slope, and into the Administration Office. Time was on my side during this errand, even if I was the first or last to hand in Mrs. Teacher's class register, I awarded myself the time I thought it would take waiting in a line of those others who carried their classrooms registers to the Administration Office, waiting for their received slip to hand back to their teacher. This was sometimes a good ten minutes and it was never questioned. I guess the responsibility merited the benefit of any doubt in Mrs. Teacher's head to my delayed return. And after all, I was rapidly becoming the teacher's new pet. Why wouldn't she trust me?

There were other classroom escape routes too: erecting the girls' netball posts, second in command to ringing the school bell signifying the start of dinner break and the end of the day, taking around my own stuff as lost property. I created a catalogue of escapism tricks to satisfy my gobbling needs.

Now, I realise I make much use of the word 'gobbling'. This is not entirely true. My use of this word perhaps depicts a scoff of the whole sandwich or at least finishing off what has been left in one quick mouthful. However I fear that I paint a poor representation of myself and of my antics back then. In some form of self searching justification for my actions many moons ago, I must interject some clarity to my use of the word 'gobbling.' I refer to this descriptive word as a means to illustrate me having to gobble what I could find before anxiety got the better of me, or I was indeed caught red-handed, like a crow hurriedly plucking at the remains of a fresh carcass before the oncoming car causes him to fly away.

For once I was nearly caught. I was nearly the dumb crow that got his timings all wrong and ended up against the grill of that oncoming car. According to Mrs. Teacher and my classmates, I was in the toilet, when in reality I was just on the other side of the far classroom wall, gobbling the remains of a tomato sauce and crisp sandwich. To be honest it wasn't much, a crust really was all it amounted to, and I was disappointed. All I had eaten that day was one of my Mars bars from my classroom tray, but the gem in this particular lunch box was that at the bottom, under the sandwiches, scrunched up foil and empty orange juice carton was a Fox's Classic bar, only one of the most luxurious biscuits of my childhood. *Something for the way home, I thought as I pocketed it into my school trousers.*

Next thing, Trevor Wigwam burst through the fire doors and into the corridor to which the box rooms of the girls and boys cloakrooms extended. Trevor's surname was actually Wixam. However, and unfortunately for Trevor, he had battled a rare medical life-threatening condition, the result of which meant he had no body hair, so he wore a wig, and his skin was that of a native American Indian, and they lived in Wigwams. Anyhow, moving on...Trevor Wigwam had barged into the open cloakroom area just as I had finished squeezing the remaining corner crust of this tomato and crisps sandwich into my mouth. Thankfully I had chosen a classmates Knight Rider bag that was hanging directly behind the fire door. I had just a second's grace to pull the brown hooded duffle coat off its peg next to me and hang its hood over my face, so the coat covered my crouched self that was kneeling on the narrow bench before the doors closed. Trevor stopped and grumbled as if he wasn't sure what toilet door to go through, and then he was gone, leaving the door to the boys' toilet to close behind him. Trevor was a gentle soul, and apart from ripping the Mickey out of his surname, and stealing his wig, and asking him if he'd ever get pubes, he wasn't bullied by the boys in our class, as we had the utmost respect for him beating death. Nevertheless, if he had looked over his shoulder behind the fire door, I think he would have had the same reaction of seeing an oversized brown rodent quivering on the cloakroom bench as perhaps a Warner Brothers cartoon character does when inflicted with the pain of being hit by a ACME sledge hammer on it big toe or paw. You know the reaction...they jump about six feet into the air and seem to hover until their eyes had receded back into their sockets, and their mouths having closed once their tongues have rolled back up off the floor and sat back in the dwelling of its mouth. Not forgetting the steam coming out of their ears with their hair standing erect on end as if electrified. Oh, forget the last response for obvious aforementioned reasons. The part that you don't see on the Warner Brothers cartoons is the character shitting itself. I think if Trevor had seen this Dr. Who-like oversized rodent perched on the cloakroom bench, Trevor would have shed his bowel content there and then. Thankfully, he didn't shit, at least not in the corridor as he didn't look behind him. He did however enter the boys' toilets, which was my moment to squeeze the lid back on the lunchbox, shove it in the Knight Rider bag, zip up the bag, remove the brown rodent-skin-like duffle coat, peg it back up and peg myself back to class.

I must admit that I don't remember craving a kiddies' elevenses or an afternoon get-me-by after that. It finished as quickly as it started, though my lunchbox thievery did stretch many weeks. The strange thing which leaves me (and most probably you; the reader of this chapter) is that nothing was ever raised to Mrs. Teacher or with the parents of my classmates whose lunchboxes I terrorised over those many weeks. I would, as I am sure you would also notice if your cling-film / tin-foiled wrapped sandwich had had a small kiddies' bite size arc out of the middle of one of the halves, or the fruit or biscuit that you were saving for the walk home had vanished. To me, at that time, this didn't seem to register on my radar. It was just about other people's food. Perhaps they were not concerned, perhaps they didn't even notice. But then again I refuse to believe that. I would have noticed so why didn't they? Why I am so quizzed about this I am not sure, what respected thief wants to be caught, hey? The truth is that I wasn't caught, obviously no harm was done and I matured during my schooling years to find that Carol Bailey's cleavage was far more awesome than my fellow classmates' lunchbox contents and great for throwing gummy bears between as her boobs pushed her top away from her chest, creating an opening of sweet delight. MMM!"

Now the most pleasant aspect of this tale of minor naughtiness is that our Geezer learnt the error of his ways. However, just as quickly he moved onto another obsession, one that was going to land him in trouble over and over again. *Boobies.* Just think what could have become of him if his passion for screwing things up with the women in his life had not overshadowed his passion for food. Yes, he could have become fat and useless instead of just useless.

Let It Pee.

Even us feeble-minded men should be able to work out for ourselves that some things are simply taboo. I mean completely and utterly no-go areas. Nope, I'm not referring to the occasional request for a bit of 'back door action' because although we may ask and beg and bribe, we know, deep down in our *own* bowels, that this just ain't ever going to happen. Remember, we are talking about the person we want to spend the rest of our lives with. Remember, this is the girl that we told the lads down at the pub that we love deeply and truly. Do we really want that girl to be the one we will always think of, even though we try our best not to, as the one who took it up trap two? No, because as obviously bad as we are, we remain, underneath it all, good men. Respectful men. And despite that reverence we show to our forever love, we still stray into waters from which we have been warned to steer clear of. Of course we do, we are men! Yes, men, the only creature on the planet that expects its mate to clean up their piss stains after them!

Julie, 26, Sustainability Officer, Dorchester.

"It's not like I'm some clean freak. I want to say that first. Or some prude. I know we're all human. Flip, I'm as human as the next one, I make mistakes. Flipping heck, if I didn't, I think my standards would be too high and I'd be all on my own. I accept that I make mistakes and I accept that he makes mistakes. I want to say that he accepts my mistakes too, of course he does, I don't want it to sound like he's a complete slob or anything, because he isn't. Flip, I'd be really unfair if I gave that impression. Jack's a great guy. I love him. I properly love him and he loves me too. He shows it in so many ways. He's really sweet, buys me flowers on our twenty-seven-month anniversary, chocolates on my half-birthday, random stuff like that, and it just makes me realise I'm lucky to have him. Just because he says, how nice is that. So when I had to speak to him about his habit, flip, it was awkward. I guess I'd better start off back at the beginning, which was about two weeks after he moved in. My place was bigger, you see, because it was farther out of town and it made sense. Now it was a slow process, for me, giving up my space, letting his stuff creep more and more around the place. It's like his Xbox. It started off connected to the television in the bedroom and then, when we bought a big flat screen one, he says he wants to see what it was like on there. Flip, it was our new toy, I wasn't going to complain, but has the Xbox gone back in the bedroom? No flipping chance. Sorry, I'm going off on one, aren't I? Anyway, two weeks after he moves in is when I first notice this little stain on the carpet in the bathroom, a good few inches way from the loo, so I work out it's not a leak. Well, not *that* sort of leak. I don't think twice and I clean it up. It goes, it comes back, I clean it, it goes... You get the picture. Now it starts to grow a bit. I don't know whether it looks worse because I've been scrubbing at the carpet a bit, using detergents and stuff, but flip, it's starting to look like a little half moon there. I'm perplexed. Of course, I don't say anything, do I? Why would I? Jack's the type of boyfriend who puts the seat and the lid down every time, so I've got no clue that he's the culprit. Until I go to the loo one day and he's, for once, not put the seat back down. Now I actually remember smiling about this at the time. I thought something like 'oh, he is human after all,' and it's as I'm about to put the seat down for myself that I step onto the stain. Flip, did I mention I wasn't wearing shoes? It's wet. Not damp. Wet! So I look down at this half moon stain, suddenly wet after Jack's been in the bathroom, and I don't know if it's the angle I'm looking down at, but it's right then I can see on the porcelain of the toilet, the actual top of the bowl, the bit the seat, well, sits on, is soaked too. I'm telling you, inside my head was like one of the clips from CSI Miami or whatever it's called. I see him standing there, his thingy out, and he's probably still listening to the television or plotting his next move on his Xbox game, and all the while his 'splash-back' is adding to that little half moon stain. Flip, it all rushes back at me. The cloth, the cleaning spray, sometimes no rubber gloves? You see? This was about more than a wet foot! I call him into the bathroom and try to talk it through with him and he's being understanding and sorry, and that just makes it worse. He grins, just a nervous smile trying to defuse the situation because he's a good guy and he doesn't like arguments, and while he's grinning I feel the words coming out of my mouth, and I know they're the wrong words, but I ask, 'Are you taking the piss?' Now, of course he was going to laugh. Then? Flip, I lost it. We have a deal now. He sits down when he goes, especially if he thinks his mind isn't on the job. Flip, he doesn't want to ruin the new laminated floor he paid for, does he?"

Julie may have been justifiably angry but it is important to note that Jack did not go out of his way to piss her off. He was just a little bit slack, lazy and lacked aiming skills. This is behaviour that is not malicious and can be modified. In fact, it can be said with some confidence that Jack is a changed man and will continue to be so for a little while longer, at least, until he finds another way of placing himself into his very own seventh circle of Hell. Which, let's be honest, we all know he will at some point. So remember Jack as you contemplate the story of Ben who, in comparison to what Jack did, could well in fact be the urinating Devil himself!

Ben, 37, Publican, Waterlooville.

"Ally's mental. Seriously mental. I've

had some stupid break ups in the past, some crazy row that went too far, stayed out too late, went to the footy when I said we were going for dinner, but what happened with me and Ally was something different. Right, so her mum was coming to visit. Not her dad, mind you, because that old gob of shite could not get his head around the fact that I stayed over, that we were all but living together, but the mum was coming to stay. So I know Ally's going to want to clean the place from top to bottom, and I'm not getting in the way of that. Look, she's not O. C. D. but she's a pain in the arse when it comes to cleaning, so I do the good boyfriend thing and volunteer to mow the lawn. So what if it takes me three times as long as it should, right? I'm out of the way, I have a couple of bottles of beer and all the jobs get done. So I pack everything away and even take my shoes off before I go inside to use the loo. Fair enough, I didn't close the bathroom door but I honestly thought she was downstairs, and then she walks past the door so I wave and say hi. And then she goes nuts. Apparently waving with both hands is some illegal manoeuvre. Okay, so it's waving with both hands while still peeing and not even looking where the pee is going that's the illegal manoeuvre, but I swear I'd thought I'd nearly finished, and it wasn't that much and I cleaned it up myself. I'm getting fucking roasted while I'm on my hands and knees scrubbing. I'm getting roasted while I'm rinsing out the cloth and then I'm getting screamed at for rinsing out the cloth in the sink. I'm getting yelled at for not putting the cloth straight in the bin and then I catch both barrels a-fucking-gain when I put the cloth in the bathroom bin and not the outside bin. In the middle of this her mother arrives, and I think it will calm her down, but she relates it all to the old cow, and all that bitch does is shake her head and give me a look like I'd pissed on *her* floor. And that's it. I'm history. Ten months of effort, dinners out and flowers down the drain cos I waved at her while I was having a slash. I suppose I'm just lucky that I wasn't taking a dump!"

Of course Julie or indeed even Ally may wish to take solace in the fact that their man is going to grow out of this habit, that he will in fact be able to slash it from their repertoire. This would at least give our women hope, that one day we will wake up and realise that it is not just common courtesy to think before we tinkle but also a simple act we can do that reduces the stresses and strains on our better half's life. So if we need evidence that life gets better we need to seek the wisdom of someone who has been there, seen it all and has a wardrobe full of t-shirts.

Gloria, 68, Retired, Swansea.

"The thing is like, life and love is all about a bit of give and take, isn't it? You don't get to my age without accepting people for just who they are. The good and the bad, see, it's what makes us the people we are. Well, that's what I like to think, like. And the thing is, because we are all a bit different, sometimes we make mistakes. But like I said, that's life, see. We all do things now and then, like, and sometimes, see, you've just got to laugh. I might have said before that my husband loves a pint or two. Not that it's a problem but he does and, well, this one night he wakes me up in the middle of the night, stumbling out of the bedroom, and I hears him going into the bathroom but I don't hear the light going on and I don't actually hear him *doing* anything, even though he leaves the door wide open. Well, he staggers back to bed and goes straight back to sleep, and I snuggle up to him and before long he's snoring and I'm drifting off along with him. The next morning, he's still out like a light and I gets up and goes through to the bathroom. I'd forgotten about his little wander in the middle of the night and when I go in there I can see that the windowsill, which is just behind the loo, is covered in water. I checks the window and it's shut tight, so I can't think what has happened. I just start cleaning it up and then I can see it's not just on the windowsill; it's all over the toilet tank, the floor and the lid of the toilet! Then it all comes rushing back to me, him off to the toilet in the middle of the night, and I realise he's, well, he's peed all over the place. Dirty bugger. Now I can see by that look in your eyes that you're wondering why the wee was all over the windowsill, aren't you? Well, let me ask you, have you ever woke up with your soldier stood to attention? Right, then. Just cos he's in his seventies doesn't mean he's still not in full working order. See, there's things that compensate for a few silly things here and there, now innit? I bet a few of the younger girls out there wish their fella could still stand proud after a few beers!"

So ladies, it would appear that this is not something your man is going to grow out of. It seems that ever since he finally mastered his potty he has secretly been yearning for the freedom to simply let loose wherever and whenever he wishes. How can you change things? That I don't know, maybe nobody knows. You can train a dog to cry at the door or fetch its leash when it needs to go. A cat will, almost without fail, not just use its designated toilet place but will also cover up the wet patch afterwards. So maybe you should aim to take pleasure in the small things. Maybe you should just rejoice when he does in fact use the facilities at all because, let's face it, there are a whole host of other far more interesting places just waiting for us to relieve our bladder.

Lance, 34, IT Consultant, Chelmsford.

"What I think is this. They're jealous. Seriously, seriously jealous because, let's be honest here, man to man as it were, we can *go* wherever we like. Can't we? Behind a bush, behind a car, in the rain, in the snow, in the wind if you position yourself carefully. It just doesn't hold us back, does it? We don't need a comfortable seat, we don't even need to squat down, we can just whip it out and we're off to go. Have knob will travel. Well, have knob will pee, anywhere, while travelling, I suppose. And that's the thing that does their head in. Now, if you're out and about with the lads, it's not a worry. You just step five yards away and turn your back, as long as there's no splash-back onto anyone's shoes, you're sorted. God, no one would even make comment. A man's gotta do what a man's gotta do and all that, right? But you bring *them* into the equation and the rules all change, and like I said, it's down to bloody-minded jealously. If *they* can't do it, *we* can't do it. No, let me be a bit more specific. If *my wife* can't do it, *I* can't do it. Hang on, I can be even more exact. If my wife *says* I can't do it, *I* can't do it! And trust me, over the years, I've done it pretty much everywhere. Got bollocked for it each and every time, of course, but first of all, by the time I get the bollocking, it's too late, the job is done. And secondly, for every time she's caught me peeing where I shouldn't, there's ten, fifteen, twenty times more that she hasn't! See, it starts off where you are out for a walk and you need to go so you quietly nip behind a tree. She's not amused but no one is around, but instead of letting it lie, she makes a big noise about it so that everyone knows what I've done anyway, cos she tells them! We were on holiday in Greece once, and I'm in the pool, and I know there's the rumour that if you pee in a pool then the water around you turns blue but trust me, years of experience tell me that's just not going to happen, so I go and then this voice echoes across from the sun lounger, 'I hope you're not doing what I think you're doing,' and of course, everyone looks my way and the threat of the blue dye is redundant because she's drawn a lot more attention to me all by herself. And then, of course, I'm the one that's shamed her! Jesus, if she'd kept her gob shut for once, half the population of Kos wouldn't have known I'd peed in the pool! But that's not the worst of it. Can you believe this? She expects me to get out of the shower if I need to take a leak. Now come on, that's just mental. I'm soaking wet, there's running water and there's a plug hole. It's not like she's in there with me and it's some kinky golden shower malarkey going on, it's just me and my pee. Anyway, it holds off athlete's foot, doesn't it? Now, the bath is a different matter, I'll give her that. I maybe would not have done it in the past but now I see her point. Okay, I'm not proud of this now but it happened a long time ago. I like to take baths, okay? It doesn't make me less of a man and sometimes I like to have bubbles. I work long hours, sitting for most of it, I go to the gym and then I seize up. So I take baths to ease it. Nothing girly, it just works. So I'm in the bath, bubbles up to my neck and sometimes I'll take my book in with me, or sometimes the wife comes in for a chat. Now, I'm as relaxed as relaxed can be in there and this one time, we're chatting away and suddenly from talking about what's for dinner over the weekend I'm met with this wall of silence and a look that would curdle milk. So I ask what's wrong and then she looks down at me and I follow her eyes and, well, the soap suds are moving away from my, let's call it my groinal area, and I've gotten so relaxed, so chilled, even with her sat on top of the toilet seat chatting to, that I've had a little wee. And will she take it as a good thing that I can be that relaxed around her? No chance. Claims she's never done it. Well maybe, maybe not, but if she did, not in the bath maybe but if she did or could just go anywhere when she needed to maybe she'd be less uptight. Never told her that, obviously. I was in enough trouble as it was."

Lance's problem, in his mind, was not what he did, but the fact that, despite being married to her, he did not fully *know* his audience. Perhaps that word, *audience*, is a key factor for a man to consider when he is considering an outdoor urination.

Julia, 43, Sales and marketing Officer, St. Helens.

"I'd been dating Perry on and off for a couple of months and neither of us were rushing things. I've got a little boy, Joe, and he was six, nearly seven at the time, so I didn't want him to meet someone, and then have that someone disappear out of his life. Again. Perry played rugby for his local team. Well, he played rugby for his local team's third team. He asked me if I wanted to go and watch, and I thought it was a great opportunity for him and Joe to meet without it being anything huge. So we go. Now, third team rugby, I realised quickly, is not a huge spectator sport. We tripled the crowd numbers, if truth be told, but Joe seemed to like it. You could really hear the effort, to be fair to them all, and then at half time the two teams stayed on the pitch and kind of huddled up in two groups, and I was watching the steam rising off these two groups of men, and I'm kind of thinking it's nice that Perry is still playing a sport he loves, and Joe points across the pitch and says, really casually, 'That man is doing a wee', and, yes, one of Perry's team mates had disengaged himself from the huddle and was peeing onto the side of the pitch about twenty yards from us. Then the player finishes doing what he's doing and he waves at us, and then I see it's not one of his team mates but actually Perry himself. We did not stay to watch the second half!"

There are many things that a man does to land himself in hot water that he well and truly knows will be frowned upon but he ways up the risk of getting caught and promptly does it anyway. However, when it comes to emptying one's bladder, there are times when a man may not even be aware that he is doing it. Or where he is doing it. Or who he is doing it on.

Carla, 43, Housewife, Bristol.

"Mark and I had been married for three years before Mark Junior came along. Everyone was naturally very excited, but Mark's younger brother, Owen, had been working away and had missed the first few weeks, so when he came to visit I had no qualms at all with the pair of them going out to wet the baby's head. To be honest, it was a chance for me to invite my mum over and just have a completely chilled out night. I didn't expect them to be as late as they were, but they weren't that drunk when they got in, and I was up feeding the baby anyway. So after a while we all go off to bed. The baby is a bit fussy for a while but finally he goes off and Mark Senior's already flat out, snoring like he used to when I thought drunk Mark was cute, and before long I drop off too. It's normally the baby that would wake me up with a wet nappy but that night it's Mark. Only of course he's an alleged adult and therefore is not wearing a nappy. But all the same, he's managed to piss while he's still asleep. All. Over. The Bed. Lovely! It's like he's purposely turned his body to face me when he's done it too, so I, even in the deepest of deep sleeps would have thought he was being sweet and cuddling up to me. So I jump out of the bed, trying to be as quiet as possible, trying to wake him up from his drunken coma, all the while trying to make sure I don't wake the baby up, and that's when I realise that the back of my pyjamas are soaked, sticking to my skin, covered in his piss, and that's when I lose it and I wake Mark, Mark Junior and Owen because I need to get a shower, RIGHT NOW and I needed them to at least make an effort to change the baby. Dirty, filthy disgusting brat. Mark senior, I mean, of course."

Carla may have had to clean up a bit of leakage but at least she didn't have to wash her whole wardrobe of clothes, which is what Jeff's girlfriend Caroline had to do after one particular over exuberant night out.

Jeff, 33, Design Technician, Peterborough.

"Okay, so the worst bit of it, like, wasn't the doing it as much. The worst bit was the, like, waking up halfway through doing it and realising just what it was I was doing. We'd been going out for a while, but I always thought she was out of my league, like, and it made me a bit, I don't know, like, insecure. So when we used to go out I'd drink a bit too much. Dutch courage, like. I had no reason to, I was basically being a bit stupid like, and it's not as if I'd get jealous or start fights or puke all over the bathroom or anything bad like that. Until the night. The night that will never ever be forgotten because she won't let me forget it, obviously. So we're out, I have a few to drink, now she does too, like, so it's not that I was steaming and she was Mother Theresa, but when we get back to her place all I want to do is crash out, so we go straight to bed and straight to sleep. No funny business, like. And as far I know that's the end of the matter until I wake up and Caroline is screaming 'Jeff! Jeff!' and I open my eyes thinking that someone has broken in, but instead I'm stood in front of her wardrobe, which is wide open, and I'm pissing like a race horse all over her clothes. The stuff on the shelves, the stuff hanging from the rail, her shoes in the bottom of the wardrobe, the lot. And she's still screaming at me and I'm still going and there's no way I can stop and now there's no way she can stop telling everyone what I've done, and whenever she's in the wrong, all she has to do is bring up the night I ruined all of her clothes by pissing in her wardrobe. Cost me a fair few quid too, but it did cure my nervous drinking habit. Cos she won't let me drink anymore."

And so the number of ways in which a man can shoot himself in the foot continues to grow. There are of course arguments that support the concept that maybe the ladies in our lives need to be a little less rigid, show some compromise but I suppose, at the end of the day, they are more than aware that the longer the rope they give us, the farther we are going to run, leaving little puddles in our wake. So while it is okay for us to urinate outdoors, indoors, wherever we like when we are with our male friends, it is best that we treat out girlfriend or wife with a great deal more respect. It's probably in everybody's best interests that we don't try to take the piss.

Gone With the Wind. The Wind in the Willows. Farts, okay?

There is very little else in life that will make a man laugh like a good fart. It is simple, mostly harmless, fun. You know, despite the claims of it being a particularly noxious brand of chemical warfare, no one's face has *actually* melted off because of a male guff. It's just a fantastically flatulent bodily function that men find funny. It really is as simple as that. Yes, it is the basest of all comedy. It is the lowest common denominator. It is Carry-On humour minus the thoughtfully crafted writing. It's the best bit of Blazing Saddles when the cowboys are sat around the camp fire eating beans. If you are a man and you don't know what I am talking about, first of all, rent the movie. Secondly, you're lying. You do know the scene and you're reading this with the missus! Huddled around that shared Kindle. You know the scene because you've done it yourself. And the best bit is that all the women have done it too. They claim they haven't but they have. Of course they have! If not, they'd explode. Or float off, or something. The difference is that they do not, would not, and would die if they did, ever draw attention to their bottom burps. We men, on the other hand, see a jolly good fart as our personal fanfare. Smell me, it announces, for I have arrived.

Most women have probably given up trying to stem their lover's stench and will gladly make do with the gentlemanly conduct of occasionally leaving the room to break wind or clenching when in company or confined spaces. More than this and even the most demanding of ladies is going to be struggling to achieve her targets. It's all about the little wins in a situation like this. But even if you are that man who walks the length of the house to ensure that she not only doesn't have to smell it but, in fact, does not even have to hear it, there will still be some deeply rooted instinct within you that will every now and then slip out and get you in trouble. You are a mere man, sub-human and mortal after all. The trick is, just don't talk about it. At your wedding. In your wedding speech.

Phil, 31, Newlywed, Middlesbrough.

"Look, I was as nervous as Hell about making a speech. I'm not the centre-of-attention type of bloke, I was never going to be

able to stand up there and reel off a load of
witty one-liners because my mind would have
just gone blank, so I was talking from the heart.
But that's better, right? To be honest when
you're the groom and you're talking about
your new bride. Talking from the heart.
Relating the things that were and are so
wonderful about her, about Wendy, the true
reasons why I married her, why I want to
spend the rest of my life with her. And the one
thing I got wrong? I didn't think it was such a
big deal, anyway. It was one sentence in a 'War
and Peace' sized epic about my feelings and
emotions and her beauty and... Seriously, I am
not laying it on thick here, my speech was a
bloody homage to her. And because it was all
'real' then it was easy for me to say, and most
importantly, it was easy for me to remember.
Okay so I get through the bit about her looks, I
get through the bit about her job and how
clever and ambitious she is, and then I just
want to throw something cute in there about
how much fun she is, how silly she can be, and
how much she makes me laugh. And I recall
this time when... Well, it led to what I thought
was a quick 'giggle' moment and it slotted into

the speech perfectly. It wasn't a lie, it wasn't exaggerated, but God damn it, I wish I'd left it out. I can't believe such a big deal has been made out of it. 'Wendy, of course, has always been able to make me laugh,' I said, taking a moment to glance at the faces of a few of her friends who were nodding in agreement. 'She's got this fantastic ability to make me laugh so hard that sometimes I do a little fart.' Well, the nodding stopped. Instantly. From the women in the room at least. Mouths dropped open. Half the blokes cracked up, in retrospect a bit too loudly because it didn't help, made it look like I'd suddenly gone all laddish, you know. Wendy hisses my name at me and I realise then that I've done something wrong, something possibly inexcusable. At that point, I can't quite work out what it is, but the rest of my speech is done for. It's like I'm talking with a mouthful of marshmallows because, not only am I trying to analyse what I've already said to spot the villain, but I'm also scanning ahead to make sure there's nothing else flammable in there. By the time it's over, I'm a wreck and I'm still getting the evil eye. What have I done? When she finally tells me, I'm actually relieved.

I thought I'd said something bad about her mum or her sister, you know, and as far as the amount of trouble I was in, I may as well have done that very thing! Apparently farts are not for discussing in public."

Of course, Phil really should have known better. When it comes to matters of the backside, men must always assume that they are living in Downton Abbey, and that anything emitted from below the waist is thus, well, below them and not to be brought up. However, even if a gent does not welcome his trump to the world with a fanfare, there are still ways in which he will give himself away and end up down wind of his lady's wrath.

Gloria, 68, Retired, Swansea.

"Now we'd be sat there, see, watching the telly or what have you, and all of a sudden there'd be this waft and I'll tell you something, it would make me gag. Now, of course, what he'd do is wrinkle up his nose and nod his chin down at the poor dog lying there on the floor at his feet. Poor little bugger took the blame for years, he did. The things is, like, I knew it wasn't the dog. See, just before the smell arrived, he'd readjust his position and do a little cough, and then he'd have that bloody grin on his face as he blamed the dog. Stupid sod thought I was daft, see. But I'll tell you who was daft! He was! He'd even blame the poor dog when the bloody thing wasn't there! But no matter what, I always knew it was him. That waft and smell and his stupid grin, so bloody pleased with himself he'd be. Dirty bugger."

To be fair, it's not like Gloria's husband raised himself off the seat, tensed every muscle in the lower half of his body, and squeezed until something that would register on the Richter scale harmonised its way out of his sphincter. Maybe, in his own way, he was trying to be subtle, attempting not to draw attention to his flatulence that he may well have been ashamed of. Except for the grin, this could well be the case. But the grin comes simply because men find farts funny. Fact. At least Gloria's husband's attempted to hide his enjoyment of his own bowel gas even if he was unable to completely stop himself from releasing it in her presence. Not all men are so considerate.

Pauline, 36, Help Line Manager, Dundee.

"We were lying in bed, so we were, just reading. I always read lying flat on my back, propped up by my pillows. Conrad reads lying on his side, with his back to me. Anyway, the way I hold the book, it means that my arms flatten the duvet down, and in the winter months it keeps the warmth in. So this one night Conrad puts his book down and turns to me quickly with a cheeky smile on his face, and I think he's only after one thing. If only, I'll tell you! All of a sudden he grabs my book and throws it on the floor, and then before I know it, the duvet is up and over my head and I'm trapped underneath, and then the smell, Jesus Christ, the smell, it hits me like it's something solid and I immediately gag. I think I'm going to puke and I can't get out from under the duvet because he's holding it tight over my head and the smell is just...and the whole time all I can hear is the muffled sound of his bloody laughter, but it's so smug sounding like he's so proud of himself. Proud of that? Disgusting little child should take a shower after that, or at least a tactical wipe!"

To be fair, there are two sides to every story.

Conrad, 38, College Lecturer, Dundee.

"Aw, come on now, eh? It was just a little Dutch Oven. Everybody's done that to their missus, haven't they, eh? The opportunity is just too good to pass up. If you can do it quiet like then she'll have no idea it's coming, and then all you've got to do is be quick to get her head under the covers, eh? That time though, eh, I'd had bad guts all night. Now, I'm honest not saying it was the dinner what she cooked, you know, but it was a tiny bit of meat and loads of veggies. Now come on, eh. What did she expect to happen? And the best bit, well, what I did was to get into bed without any pyjama trousers or boxer shorts on, because, well, I'd already smelt what I was producing in the toilet, eh. I didn't want anything to filter that out so I had me bare backside ready to do the job. And that's the best bit, eh. Because when she starts struggling and trying to get out from under the covers, I've got to twist around, and I've got the giggles now. And the giggles, well they just loosen my control, and then just as Pauline's face slaps straight into my backside, out pops another guff, eh, only this one, well, I'm laughing too much and I've got no control and it's as loud as loud can be, and well..."

Conrad is unable to continue. His laughing is not even tempered by the stern glare he is receiving from Pauline. It has to be said that he's not even trying to stop his laughter or to even hide it.

Pauline, 36, Help Line Manager, Dundee.

"Seriously, Conrad. You're thirty-eight. Thirty-eight!"

There are some men out there who are prepared to take a much more hands-on approach to paving their own way to the relationship gas chamber. What a small but, apparently, growing faction of the male species is prepared to do in the name of a laugh makes Conrad look like the purest of gentlemen. The Dutch Oven, at least, takes place in the comfort of one's own home. When it has happened once, of course, it puts the lady of the house on the back foot for evermore, always expecting it, never sure of when it will strike again. However, she knows this is not something that can ruin her day while watching television, or shopping or sat at her desk in work. For such times there is the mobile version of the Dutch Oven. Something more compact in size yet so much more intense in pungency.

Bradley, 25, Sports Development Officer, Loughborough.

"You've never heard of a Cup Cake? And I mean Cup Cake in the way that I mean Cup Cake. Right, first off, this ain't something that should ever be done to your girlfriend. You might do it to your mate. You might do it to someone you play sport with, right? But seriously. You. Do. Not. Do. This. To. Your. Girlfriend. But every single one of us does. It's like you've Cup Caked your best mate, you've liked the outcome, and then you're hooked. You have to do it any chance you get. And before you know it, you're lining one up for your girlfriend. Basically, you fart into your hand, close your hand into a fist so you seal the smell in, then you place it over your victim's face and open the hand, releasing the smell. The best thing is that no one can ever see it coming. No one expects it. It's like the Spanish fucking Inquisition! But don't do it, man. Your girlfriend will be so pissed off with you, I mean it. I've experienced it. And the worst thing...it becomes such a habit, farting in your hand, that even if you're alone, and you can feel the pressure building, then you'll actually set yourself up to Cup Cake yourself just for fun. I don't know what all the fuss is about with farts anyway. You know what a fart really is? A fart is a message from the brain to say there's a turd on the very next train? It's good, isn't it? My ex-girlfriend used to hate that poem."

Maybe the key to Bradley's use of the Cup Cake and his interest in the secret messages of the fart lies in that simplest of prefixes: ex. However, there are men out there whose rear end puts them in danger of the dog house even though they are trying their best to keep it under control and to behave in a way that should ingratiate themselves to their loved one. Some men, poor souls, simply cannot win.

Eleanor, 32, Radio Producer, Cheshire.

"Brian is a proper gym head. Totally committed, four five times a week minimum. And he plays football every Sunday. Look, we've been together for years, we don't need to spend every minute together, and I'm glad that he's got a hobby, even if it almost borders upon an obsession. He has those protein shakes a couple of times a day and this horrible looking purple stuff when he gets back from the gym. I spend a lot of time listening to music. I have to, because it's my job, but I love music too, so it's a great trade off. He goes to the gym. I listen to music. It's a really nice balance. The only difference is that my passion doesn't fill the flat with a continual and permeating general smell of fart. It's not his diet. We eat the same things. He's not a boozer so it's not like there's a reaction in his stomach to ten pints of Guinness going on, so it's just got to be those powdered drinks he makes. If I go into the bathroom after him there's this metallic stench. It's clingy. In the air, it's clingy. It feels like it's real. Like a malevolent entity in a Stephen King story. Even though he sprays air freshener, it's still there. Waiting to get me! And we'll be sat watching television or just chatting or whatever and he'll maybe get up to make a cup of coffee or something and in the space where he's been sat there'll just be this life force of fart smell emanating towards my nostrils. And, like I said, it clings. He could sit in the same place all night and not actually fart. We could go to bed and the next morning I could sit down where he'd be sat and the smell would still be there. I know it's a good thing that he's into being healthy and fit, and don't get me wrong, he does look fantastic, but I just wish he'd ditch his fart powders and fart drinks, and then we could both enjoy his exercise regime without fear of being choked to death by some cloud of noxious Brian egg arse gas. Look, some of the music I listen to stinks, I accept that. The difference is, when I press the stop button, it stops stinking. Simple as that."

It's very easy, of course, to assume that the fart is the realm of the man, and the man alone, and that woman-kind has never allowed their bodily functions to embarrass them. Now, the man who wishes to remain in the realms of the good where regular sex is pretty much the norm may wish to subscribe to this point of view. If we hear our partner emit a bum squeak, we never let them know we heard a single thing. We do not react to it. We do not giggle. We do not offer to pull their finger to make sure they got it all out. We do not tell our friends. We do not tell their friends. We forget it ever happened. But what if we only suspect? What if we have a suspicion that something has taken place that may not have been altogether planned? And what then if they choose to confess, to put the words that we are fighting so hard to keep down out there for us to hear, almost inviting us to make the words public knowledge? What then? Well then, too, we shut up. We don't mock. We don't repeat. Whatever we do, we don't repeat. Ever. Of course we don't.

Kirk, 29, Musician, Melbourne.

"So I'd not moved over to the UK for very long and I start dating this girl. She was a couple of years older than me but she was cool. The thing was, right, was that I didn't have any transport and that I was meeting people all the time, so the opportunity to go out on the beers was there all the time. Now she didn't mind and a lot of the time she'd actually come and pick me up after I'd been out on the sauce because, well, she liked me to stay over. A lot, if you know what I mean. So this one night, I'm out in town and we had no plans to meet up, and I'm just starting to walk home and it's freezing. Like seriously freezing. And I've not properly acclimatised yet, so I calls her up and asks her if she wants to warm me up, you know what I mean? So, of course, she says yes and says she's on her way. Anyway before too long I see her driving along the street, and she's got the front windows open, and when I get in I can see she's freezing and got a look like hell on her face, so I think maybe she didn't want to come and pick me up. I get her to close the windows while we're still parked up, and then this smell hits me. It's like an underpinning stench of sewage, man. It made my fucking eyes water. It smelt like someone had shit in her car, man. So without thinking I ask her, what the fuck is that smell? And it's like I've opened this floodgate of truth, and I swear to God, I wish I never asked because I didn't want to be responsible for storing the knowledge that she was about to impart to me. Turns out, when I'd phoned, that she was just about to go to the toilet. And not for a leak. Yeah, for the other one. Not one, as such, more a number two. Well, it wasn't a desperate situation, and she didn't want to think of me out in the cold, so she left there and then, planning to sort out her business when she got back. Well the thing was, the sitting position of driving convinced her body that she was ready to make some brown so, and these are her words, not mine, she starts to unleash this succession of death farts. Of course by the time she sees me waiting in the road, the car reeks and all she can think of to do is open the windows. And she's sat there telling me all this, still in need of a shit and still dropping fart bombs. By the time we got back to her place the car stank like a cow shed. Needless to say, neither of us was up for too much sex action that night."

Kirk, despite not mocking his girlfriend, not laughing in her face and not making a big deal of it, still ended up single the following week. Had he been able to keep his mouth shut after the event? Had he in fact made the fatal mistake of telling everyone both he and she knew about the incident?

Maria, 31, Office Manager, London.
"Of course he did, the stupid Australian wanker!"

Shake it up baby now.

A man is seldom alone with his thoughts. Simply, it doesn't suit him. It's very unlikely that a man will take time in his day to ponder the inner most workings of his mind, to probe why he feels the emotions he does and to analyse what he may do in order to enhance the experience that is life. If a man is going to take any time during the day to think about anything then that topic is, stereotypically but also very true, sex. And, of course, it does not take an astrophysicist to work out that if you leave a man whose wandering mind more often than not refocuses itself on sex alone for any length of time, he is invariably going to end up having sex with his favourite and most considerate partner. Himself.

Now, taking his pleasure literally into his own hands does not fill a man with guilt. This is not cheating. Of course it's not. There's no one else there so how could it be? If anything, he's actually being the least selfish he can be. He's in the mood. She may be in the mood, she may not be in the mood. Now, if he makes it apparent that he's up for a bit of sexual shenanigans and she's not, then she may feel bad. She may feel she has to make the effort. Either way, this could have an impact upon the overall mood and ambience of the relationship so, in the plodding and irresponsibly logical part of the man's mind, simply sorting himself out is actually the best thing he can do for the pair of them. For the most part, the wife or girlfriend has no problem with this very intimate part of their man's routine. They know it is going to happen so why both fighting it, right? What they do object to, and what will of course plunge their handy man into hot water, is the fall out, the residue if you will, from their man's bashful behaviour. And no, I don't mean what you're thinking. That's just disgusting. What I mean is that although our women accept it goes on, they don't want it thrust in their faces. All they want to know is that if we're going to indulge in the five knuckle shuffle then we'll do it subtly so they don't actually have to admit to knowing anything about it.

Unfortunately, this simple rule is one that we men struggle to obey even though it is very likely that we should have learnt the importance of discretion at a much earlier point in our lives.

Alun, 47, Entrepreneur, Neath.

"It's still the thing to this day that makes me hang my head in shame. And you know what, I swear to God that until today, I've never said a word about it to anyone. Not a soul. Why would I? Thankfully, no one else has talked about it either, at least as far as I know, and knowing my family, if they'd have talked about it I'd have found out because they'd have taken the Mickey out of me right to my face. Okay, so I was in the second year of my 'A' levels, so I was, I guess, seventeen or eighteen. No, there's no guessing about it. I was eighteen. I'd been eighteen for exactly two weeks when it happened. You don't forget the detail of an event like this, trust me. I was at a college for my 'A' levels as opposed to school, so quite often during a particular day I'd have a lot of free time. On the day in question I had one class first thing in the morning for a couple of hours and then the rest of the day was free. I was up to speed on all of my work so I went home. When I got there, no one was in. Okay, it *seemed* like no one was in. In my house, at that age, it was rare that the house was empty. If you wanted to, umm, have any alone time fun, it was often a rushed and hurried act that was more about shame than it was about pleasure. And now here I was, the house at my mercy. What else was an eighteen-year-old boy going to do? So I lay back on my bed, close my eyes and... and it's only just after the moment of release, as it were, that I open my eyes and I look up and my bedroom door being pulled silently closed as someone beats a surreptitious retreat from my room. I thought I was going to die. Seriously, seriously die. I could feel my heart pounding not just in my chest but in my ears, and yes, in my rapidly becoming flaccid penis. I make sure the door is fully shut and then I clean myself up and then I just sit on the end of my bed, wondering which family member it was. Half an hour later my mum shouts up to ask if I want a cup of tea. If it had been my dad, we could have had a man to man chat. If it had been my brother, I could have bribed him not to tell anyone. But my mum? How was I meant to broach this with my mum? I don't know now and I didn't know then. So guess what? We've never talked about it. Thank God!"

Had Alun ever had the nerve to discuss this somewhat unsavoury incident with his mother he probably would have found her to be understanding. As we've already said, this is one activity that women know takes place and are happy with it as long as it is done in an appropriate place, so Alun, choosing to entertain himself with a little daytime tug was not actually breaking the rules. Had his mother walked in on him playing with himself in the living room while watching the home movie of Grandma's eighty-fifth birthday party while the dog licked peanut butter off his nuts, then he may have been in trouble. As it was, maybe she was more worried about whether he was angry that she'd not knocked while he knocked one out. Alun need not worry. He'd done nothing to draw attention to his handiwork. If only all men were so thoughtful.

Suzanne, 31, Teacher, Worksop.

"Greg had been out with his mates. It was a Friday night and I'd been really busy in work, and I was actually looking forward to an early night. When he gets in, I've got to be fair, he's trying to be really quiet, but when he's had a few drinks he's like Bambi on ice. But he's trying, so even though he wakes me up,

I'm not bothered at all. I ask him if he's had a good time, he asks what I watched on television, and then, of course, he makes a drunken suggestion, seeing I'm awake now. I manage to deflect him and he's fine and says he's off to get a coffee and maybe see if there's any sport highlights on. Off he goes and off I go straight back to sleep. Next morning he's still snoring away when I get up, and I make some breakfast for myself and sit down to watch Saturday Kitchen. I notice that the little red light on the telly is still on and that the Sky system is still powered up, so I use the remote and turn the television on, and I can't believe what I'm seeing. It's not long before ten on a Saturday morning, and there's some skanky, orange tanned slapper with a low cut top talking on the phone while wiggling suggestively at the camera. I can't work out what's going on until it hits me. The last thing Greg was *watching*! The last thing Greg was *doing* before he came to bed! Then I see across the bottom of the screen there's a phone number to ring and I realise that the slapper on the screen is talking to someone while they're... while they're pleasuring themselves! So I pick up the phone and hit redial. When my mother answers, who I'd phoned the night before I'm relieved that I have to make up some stupid excuse for why I called her. So, at least, I know he was just watching and not having someone talk him through is hand job! That does take the edge off my mood, though, but I still had him out of bed within the next ten minutes, hangover or no hangover. If he's going to do it to himself he may as well have some dignity, not bashing his Bishop as some over-the-hill glamour model pretends to felate her telephone! Disgusting!"

When Greg hears Suzanne's take on the tale of his faux pas he is even more relived than ever.

Greg, 31, Factory Supervisor, Worksop.

"She checked the phone? Shit, I never knew that! Thank fuck I used my mobile. Straight up though, it was the first time I phoned and I've not phoned since, but I get about ten text messages from them a week. 'Filthy Fiona is waiting for your call now.' 'Dirty Diana wants to listen to you as you touch yourself. Call her now.' I'm quick to delete them but I'll be even more careful now. Since I got my smart phone pictures come through as well. Mind you, it could have been worse. My mate was doing the same, he didn't phone in but was watching the late night one, because they actually get their kit right off like, and he fell asleep afterwards. Well his missus came downstairs to bring him to bed, and he's left the telly on and he's got his cock in his hand still. He was in a lot more trouble than me though, I've got to say."

Given the way in which men fail do to anything else well but incriminate themselves, it is a massive surprise that there are, in fact, any crimes perpetrated by the male gender that are not immediately punished. This is even more pertinent when playing with their penises is the crime. Even if they do not get caught mid-stroke then they are bound to forget something, a vital element that will come back to haunt them. I'm not talking about something gross like not wiping up the residue. That is something that's learnt at a very early age and never leaves us. It only takes a parent holding up one crusty sock with an appalled look of fear etched across her face for that lesson to be imprinted forever.

It's more the material that brings about the need to clean up the residue that gives away his guilty pleasure.

Gerry, 28, Paramedic, Stockport.

"It was about four weeks after the wedding and the in-laws were coming over to watch the wedding DVD. It was nothing fancy. We hadn't even planned to record it but Michelle's brother had recently bought a pretty good camera and offered to tape the speeches at least. We'd have had to jump through hoops to have the ceremony recorded, but we both thought that, at least, having some of it preserved would be nice. To be fair, he'd done a good job, put some music at the start over the titles. We'd already watched it two or three times ourselves, and this was the first time anyone else was going to see it, so Michelle especially was quite excited. So when they arrive I'm getting everyone a drink and Michelle wants to start the show straight away, and I tell her I'll do it because I know she struggles to use the Xbox controller to play disks because, to be fair, the buttons aren't labelled. She tells me not to worry because she'll actually play it through the DVD player for once, and I know she can do that, so I crack on with the drinks, and then she properly shrieks my name, so I charge into the living room where she's stood in front of her parents, and she's got a disk in her hand, and I can see the DVD player is open, but it's only when she asks me 'What the hell is this?" do I focus on the disk and the words written across it 'Sodomania Slop Shots 6' and it's then I know I'm right in the shit. There's no way she's going to believe me when I say I haven't watched it in months because it's right there in the player, right? Her mother keeps asking, 'What is it? What is it?' and despite her dad being a right miserable twat, I can see the edges of his mouth curling up into a grin that tells me he either secretly hates me and is glad to see me get my comeuppance, or he's a big fan of the Sodomania Slop Shot series! I'd totally forgotten I'd even had the film, let alone that it was in the DVD player, but that line of defence was never going to work. We never did watch the wedding film with the in-laws. I think it is too painful a memory for us all. Except for my father in law. I know he's still grinning!"

To be fair, Gerry got off pretty lightly. For the men reading, (boys, grab hold of the Kindle now) take a second to consider how your partner would have reacted if she'd found hard core anal sex/ cumshot porn in the DVD player during a visit from her parents. Ladies? (Pass the Kindle back, fellas) How deep back up inside would you have kneed his nuts? Despite technology, in the minds of men at least, being the realm of alpha male it is his undoing in so many different ways. Back in the old days all he had to do was hide his porn magazine in his tool box or next to the motor oil. It was a simpler time. Now he has to make sure he's cleared his cache, hidden his history and deleted his data to ensure he is not snared as a sick sexual pervert.

Ellie, 33, Workplace Health Advisor, Hastings.

"It's not often I have to use the family laptop. I have my own work computer and I've got one of these fancy token devices that allows me to access me work emails and the Internet from home, so basically it's his to use whenever he likes. But it was one Saturday afternoon when one of my friends came over for a coffee, and she mentions that the photographs from a wedding we'd been to were up online. Jonny, my husband, had been using the computer, so it's all ready to go, so I suggest we have a look. I open up the Internet and she tells me the web-address. I remember it perfectly. The usual three Ws and then CliffordWrightPhotography.co.uk it was. So we take a seat in front of the keyboard and I type 'www.cl' and that is as far as I get because the drop down thingy which shows previous web-address that start the same way appears on the screen and we are both speechless. Me and my friend. My friend who is a bit of a gossip to be honest. Staring at this list of web-sites that my husband has obviously been indulging himself with. Clit lickers. Clit lovers Clunge. You name it, it's there. Who would have thought that 'cl' was the gateway to so much smut? And we're sat there having to look at this list of websites! Neither of us finds it funny, and I hope that one of us will, but the only change of expression I see is on her face tells me everyone is going to *know* about this within an hour. And, of course, I'll get painted as the ice queen who never puts out and has forced her husband to sort himself out while looking at Internet porn sites. Turns out half the time this is what he'd be looking at while I was at the other end of the table working on my own laptop! Made me feel sick it did. Anyway after my friend left I had a proper look at the sites. Don't tell him, obviously, but some of them were pretty good!"

Now, Ellie's grin as she finished her little tale told me two things. The first was that she, underneath the hurt and appalled exterior, had no real problem with her husband looking at porn on the Internet but would rather he didn't do it when she was right there. The second was that since she'd uncovered Jonny's dirty secret she had herself taken to 'enjoying' the sites in more ways than one. Of course, only a man could take this situation and ruin it.

Jonny, 35, Trading Standards Officer, Hastings.

"Of course I don't mind if she does that. Of course I don't, she can do what she likes, especially if she'll let me watch."

The older generation has a different approach to the situation of course.

Gloria, 68, Retired, Swansea.

"He's always done it, he has. Well, not so much the last few years, like, but then he's getting on a bit. The way I sees it is this, see, leave him to it. Because the thing is, if he's busy bothering with himself then he's not bothering me. Gives me a bit of peace to have a nice cup of tea."

Memoir of a Geezer

Now I bet you are wondering if our geezer has an appropriate story to follow on from the last topic. Of course he has. The most difficult issue was deciding which of his memoirs to use. There were plenty from when he was younger, of course, like having to explain why a certain patch of carpet in his bedroom was a different colour and texture than the rest. Or the many places he has hidden his porn stash over the years, whether they be in paper, VHS, DVD or on-line format, and how, even in the digital age, he's still managed to stick things together. But the one that epitomises his amazing skill of doing wrong even when he is trying his hardest to do right is a short but not-so-sweet tale from his early twenties, which, of course, resulted in him being once more single. It's a useful anecdote to have in hand, if you will.

Shake it up baby now.

"Three months it took me to get a date with her, three months of playing the game, of trying to be smooth, of giving it my all. And I'll tell you what, once I actually got the date, I was even better. Not kidding. I was like Pierce Brosnan when he was still good with a little bit of Daniel Craig thrown in there for good luck. She was both shaken and stirred, all in the good way too. Unfortunately it all fell to pieces when it was me that was shaken. By myself.

Hot as the proverbial she was. Out of my league, I'll admit that, and maybe that is what I needed. As a twenty-two-year-old I thought I was the dog's bollocks but I really wasn't, so to have this uber-hotty make me work to even let me buy her dinner was probably exactly what I needed. I was not going to screw this up. The thing was, as time crept along slower than a snail it became screamingly, ball-bustlingly apparent that I wasn't going to get to screw her either. She had personal beliefs that I didn't challenge or push, and I suddenly found that daily, often twice-thrice daily, showers to uphold my 'hygiene' became, pardon the pun, were a God send!

The thing is she loved to kiss and when we were kissing then she had no problem with my hands wandering a little bit, but when my hands wandered a little bit then my penis grew a little bit, and when my penis grew a little bit, the pressure in my nuts would grow more than a little bit, and if I didn't have a release valve then I'd be walking like a cowboy after a long day out on the range. How and where was I meant to relieve said pressure build up if, for example, I was spending the weekend at her place and we were pretty much together twenty four seven? The answer became an obvious one. Yes, the shower. It's not like I was wasting any time in there. I was twenty-two. He stood to attention on demand, and it amazed me how much, well, *stuff* I was able to produce on a daily, if not hourly basis. The thing was, she thought I was being the cleanest, most considerate boyfriend in the world when, actually, I was in the shower, working up a lather and thinking about doing the filthiest things to her. She had no idea why I was always so happy and so sleepy all of the time although a little part of me, and not the little part you are thinking of, wondered whether she actually knew what I was up to and kind of liked it.

That was my first thought on the way to failure. Thinking that she was thinking that me thinking about her while cracking one out was okay. Thinking that it was okay for me to be spanking the monkey in her shower on an almost daily basis. Thoughts, of course, lead to actions, and my next fateful decision was to decide that locking the bathroom door, when I was showering, at least, was no longer a key element of my alone time. It's not like she was ever going to join me (although this hope did burn away at the back of my scrotum) and she'd certainly never use the loo when I was in there.

Of course, what I never considered is that she wouldn't realise that I was in there in the first place. That she would think that maybe one of us had left the shower running. And I never dreamt for a minute that she'd whip back the shower curtain at the exact point of critical mass, and I'd be leaning back against the tiles, cock in hand, eyes partially closed (thinking of her, at least...although she was even less impressed to hear that little gem of information) and sending an arc of white sticky goo through the steamy air and onto the wall opposite.

"What the heck do you think you're doing?" she screamed.

It looked to me like it was pretty obvious what I was doing as I stood there, soaped up and rapidly deflating penis in hand.

"Well?"

"I was having a wank," I said, possibly sounding more morose than I'd ever sounded in my life before.

"That's disgusting, that's..." she began to rant until she saw my deposit sliming its way down the shower wall. "That's what that is!" she bellowed. "I've been cleaning that up for weeks and I thought there was a problem with the shower! You disgusting freak! Get out! Get out!"

I knew it was not the time to try to explain myself so I quickly rinsed the soap off of me and dried off. By the time I got to her room, my stuff had all been jammed into a couple of plastic carrier bags. She made it very clear that no explanation was welcome, and that I was never to darken her door, or soil her shower, again. I bumped into her about two years later, just walking down the road, and the look she gave me...it was like I was some sort of sex offender. Seriously. All I was doing was giving myself a little bit of a treat. In her shower. The thing is, if I'd have caught her doing it in my shower, well, let's just say I'd have needed a shower all of my own!"

So our Geezer got himself dumped while getting himself pumped. Oh, the poetic justice. It has been good to learn of course that he's learnt self control and discipline as he has matured and developed as an individual, just as all men do as they progress through life. Or, more likely, he double checks he's locked the door before he knocks one out these days.

Everything we do and everything we say.

There are a whole host, a plethora if you will, of indiscretions and misdemeanours that men inflict upon the love of their lives that do not fit comfortably into any particular box. Like giggling at the use of the word box. Basically it is best to assume that every single thought, word or deed that escapes from our minds and becomes tangible has the potential to transform a winning situation immediately into a relegation dogfight. It doesn't have to involve the penis, pooh or porn, liquor, lingerie or lunch boxes. It's not as neat and tidy as that. There are dozens of random events just waiting to trip us up.

There are plenty of pitfalls waiting for men to walk into. And, trust me, walk right in they will. What is surprising is how soon into a relationship a man can screw it up. Surely no one can be anything else except completely focussed on their first date, right? We, as much as you, would love that to be true. Alas, more often than you would think, it is not.

Jo, 27, Artist, Stirling.

"I'd been single for a little while and it didn't really bother me, but it bothered one of my friends who was obsessed with setting me up on blind dates. I managed to get out of quite a few of them, but then this one day I get a phone call out of the blue from one of her workmates, and he's honest about the reason for his call, and he's polite, and it doesn't feel awkward, you know? Given I'm working, he's working and he's taken five minutes to give me a call and ask me out. Not too bad so I suggest he gives me a call that evening and he does and then after chatting for about half an hour I agree to meet him for a date the following night. He's promised he's not got any weird piercings or peculiar skin conditions so I thought, why not? We arrange to meet by the University, which is where he works, sorry, I should have said. He's called James and he's got a science Doctorate. So I get dressed up, making a real effort, not sure what he's got planned for the evening and off I go. Well, when I get there I have to bite my tongue a little bit because he's wearing scruffy jeans and a waterproof jacket, and he's carrying a ruck sack that may have been older than either of us. To be fair, he explains he's not long finished work and he was worried that if he'd gone to get changed then he may have been late. Considerate, I thought. I remember thinking it clearly. At the time. 'So where are we off to?' I ask, full of hope and youthful romance. 'The student union,' he says with a shrug. Pints are only a pound, he informs me. And, lucky me, it's only around the corner. Romance. Dead. And it's not just that. I'd assumed we'd be going for food so I'd not eaten. I was being expected to sink pints on an empty stomach. But I dug in. It couldn't get any worse. Could it? Now, to be fair, we had a real laugh and we had a lot in common. I mean a lot. It was, geography aside, a pretty good first date. Bit of a gent underneath the water proof jacket and scruffy jeans. So it's time to go and we step outside and it's just starting to rain. There's a taxi with its light on heading our way and James flags it down. As it pulls up he opens the door, kisses me on the cheek and tells me that he had a great time and that he'll call me the next day. I smile coyly and watch as he jumps into the taxi, smiles at me, closes the door and heads off home. Did I mention it was raining? What an idiot, eh? Still married him though. So I can remind him about our first date every single day!"

Even if a man survives a first date with his reputation still somehow intact, it is not to say that his dating disaster is not looming just around the corner. All it takes is a break from the norm, a step outside of the comfort zone and, assuming there has actually already been some, all the good work he has put in comes to nought as the house of cards he has built in the shape of a relationship comes tumbling down faster than he could ever dream that she would drop her pants. He may have planned to behave, in fact, he probably was *trying* to be the perfect gentleman, but, as we have already firmly established, it takes little more than a nudge for all the good intentions in the world to vanish quicker than the sigh of a departing partner.

Claire, 27, Dietitian, Minehead.

"Alfie and I met through work when I was doing some clinics in the community. The first few dates were really good fun. Easy almost. He let me decide what we did so I was never out of my comfort zone. And then he springs it on me. His tennis club is having a formal dinner. A James Bond night as he called it because there was a dinner, a band and a mini-casino, all to raise money for the club. It was something that he really couldn't miss because he had been the club coach and he played in their first team. He was quite sweet and romantic when he asked me, too, said that he was looking forward seeing me dressed up in a fancy dress like a proper Bondesque femme fatale. He picks me up and he looks the part, dinner jacket, bow tie, shirt immaculately ironed. I can genuinely feel my heart miss a beat. We arrive at the hotel where the dinner is being held and it looks fabulous. He opens the car door for me and holds my hand as he escorts me in. He introduces me to a few people and then we run into a bunch of middle-aged men who he used to coach tennis to. It is clear that this lot and Alfie have a good rapport, and when he orders the first one to 'drop and give me ten' it was quite funny. By the time he'd ordered the twentieth guest, in full tuxedo, the pump out some press ups, I was a little bit bored. But then he drops the macho act; he's all attentive again, and we sit down for the meal. He's making sensible conversation and I start to think that he was just playing a part in front of his boys. I had been starting to worry that it had been me on the receiving end of the act, but you can understand that, right? So just as dessert is being served, he notices that my drink is empty and literally sprints to the bar. He is taking this 'being Bond' thing to the max and I am very, very impressed. The waiter arrives and places a white plate with a perfectly moulded raspberry mousse in front of me and I have to tell him there is actually someone sat at the empty seat. If only I hadn't! Alfie arrives with my drink, sees the mousse and this absolutely mental look appears across his face. 'Watch this boys,' he announces to his cronies, and without sitting down, he slaps his face straight down into the dessert. He slurps and snorts the mousse down in about thirty seconds and finishes up by licking the plate clean. He hasn't even used his hand for balance, and his mates are all cheering, and then he looks up and grins at me, and he's got bright pink mousse all across his teeth, over his face; it's even running out of his nostrils! It's in his hair. It's on his earlobe. It's on his fucking earlobe! How much of a pig have you got to be to get mousse on your fucking earlobe? All that promise from the first few dates disappeared out the window in about, yeah, thirty seconds flat. I felt like I should have sued him under the trade descriptions act. The deal breaking night and he behaves with nowhere near as much class as he'd done before. Obviously I didn't see him again. He was quite disappointed as it happens. He was more disappointed when I told him, as I got into a taxi alone to go home, that tonight was going to be *the* night and that I was wearing underwear that would have made Pussy Galore blush."

Alfie, however, has no hesitation in admitting he made a mistake.

Alfie, 29, Former Tennis Coach, Minehead.

"School boy error, wasn't it? Should never have taken her to that dinner."

It will come as no surprise, whether you are male or female, that Alfie remains single to this day.

He may have been able to salvage the relationship with a bunch of flowers, a box of chocolates and some genuine James Bond charm the next day. Instead he chose to slide the blame across to Claire. Now, there may be the rare and occasional time when it will be the lady who is in the wrong. I stress that this occurrence is far from routine, and maybe that is why men do not know how to behave when this phenomenon manifests itself. Only a man could get it wrong when it is in fact his partner who is the one far from right.

Jan, 26, Driving Instructor, Kendal.

"We both love movies. It was one of the things that drew us to each other in the first place. And you know what? It worked out to be a real positive for us because when the kids came and we weren't going out as much, our love of films gave us 'date nights' without even leaving the house. Perfect. Matty was never a big 'pub with the lads' lad, you know, and it was just right. Turns out that his best mate married my best mate, something I'd like to take a bit of credit for, obviously, and when they had kids, too, we used to do movie nights. The kids would play and we'd watch a film.

Stress free. If the kids messed about or played up, all we had to do was press pause, sort it out, and press play again. Seriously stress free. So this one evening, we're all over at Pete and Sally's place and we're going to watch 'No Country For Old Men.' It's a film we've all been looking forward to seeing, and the kids are on best behaviour, playing in the other room. Just as the film gets going Pete excuses himself to take some popcorn through for the kids, and while he's out Matty says, very matter of factly, 'Josh Brolin. God, remember him in The Goonies?' Sally shrugs but I disagree with him. 'No way was Josh Brolin in The Goonies,' I tell him. 'Sean Astin,' I say, 'Sean Astin from Lord of the Rings was in The Goonies.' 'Yes, he was,' Matty explains, pointing at the screen. 'But so was *he*. He was the older brother.' I am having none of it and then Pete comes back in and before I have chance to say anything, Matty asks him, 'Josh Brolin was in The Goonies, right?' I'll let him tell you the rest. Just look at him. He can hardly stop himself from dancing!"

The grin on Matty's face is not helping his

cause. He's got himself in trouble over this once, and he's in a rush to make it two from two.

Matty, 30, Insurance Broker, Kendal.

"Sorry, babe, but when you're right, you're right. Or rather when *you're* wrong... Anyway, Pedro, Pete that is, comes back in and I ask him, 'Josh Brolin was in The Goonies, right?' because, unlike madam here, Pedro knows his films. There's no pause. 'Yeah, of course,' he says. 'He played the older brother, Brandon.' I look Jan right in the eye, pull a dramatic power ballad air grab, point at my crotch and utter the now immortal words, 'Blow job for Matty!" We were out of there and home before me and the kids knew what was going on. Frosty is not the word for it. It was only a joke. A throw away comment. At the end of the day I'm right so little of the time that I got carried away, over-excited. Trust me, I'm really sorry. I was really looking forward to that film and I've still not had a chance to see the end of it."

It would appear that Jan has been waiting for that line from Matty for quite some time.

Jan, 26, Driving Instructor, Kendal.

"Yeah, and funnily enough you've still not had that blow job either, have you?"

Matty is clearly suffering on the back of his throwaway comment, and it is so often the case that a particularly unsubtle one-liner will upset the apple cart. More often than not, to be fair to man in general, the words that inflict the damage will not have been premeditated to cause offence. It is more likely to be a moment of thoughtlessness as opposed to arrogance or ignorance that will see tepid water rapidly boiling over.

Cindy, 28, Full Time Mum, Bury St Edmunds.

"When I was pregnant, Alec was simply incredible. He could not do enough for me. Especially when I went through a bit of a cravings phase. It wasn't massive and it wasn't like I wanted bizarre things, but basically, what it boiled down to was whatever it was I had a taste for I'd really, really want for, like, a week. One of those things was Alec's chilli. I've always liked it, but for that week when I was craving it, I could have eaten it morning, noon and night. And, let's be honest here, I did eat it morning, noon and night. Alec was patient and would cook up batch after batch, day after day. One evening he made an absolute vat of it and put a good few portions in the freezer. Smart man, my Alec. Mostly. So one evening, I've not even asked but he's offered to microwave me a bowl of chilli, and he is bang on the money. My mouth starts salivating immediately. He heats it through in the microwave, takes it out to stir it and realises it's bubbled over and spilt down the sides of the bowl. Now, he wasn't trying to be clever. He wasn't trying to be funny. He didn't even say it that loud, but said it he did, and I heard it. What did he say? What did he mutter as he wiped up the spill? What did he say that made me sick to my stomach, sick to my unborn baby and unable to ever even think about eating his chilli again? I'll tell you. He takes a wad of kitchen towel, swipes it across the inside of the microwave, looks at it and then he says, 'Wiping up chilli sauce is just like wiping your arse, isn't it?' Why could he not just have kept his mouth shut, eh?"

So it would appear that even when a man is on

a good run, earning potentially vital bonus points as he charges for the line, he still has that undeniably male ability to ruin it. For the most part, it will be something that spills out of his mouth, unbridled and probably, in all honesty, un-thought, that zaps him from not as far from hero as he usually is to zero in an instant. Of course, such impressive looking form can be destroyed with a single act too. It doesn't have to be all verbal. And it doesn't have to be anything vindictive either. Stupid, yes. Obviously. Just not vindictive.

Stan, 32, Landlord, Salford.

"The christening had been a lovely day. Up until that point. Alison had been, in the build up to it, quite stressed, so I'd got stuck in, and while she sorted everything at the church, I arranged everything at the reception afterwards. We'd invited a lot of family and friends, and I was more than aware that between them they had a lot of kids. So with that in mind, I'd booked a big bouncy castle for out the back of the pub, and we were lucky enough to have cracking weather so the kids were out there having fun. The only problem was that one of Alison's aunts was late, she'd missed the ceremony, and it was really getting to Alison's family. I will confess to you that I didn't give a shit. Apparently, she was the family cow. She'd not come to the wedding and I'd never met her, so I was totally oblivious to what all the fuss was about. Anyway, with or without this so called bloody special guest, the day was perfect. I was earning all sorts of plaudits from Alison for looking after the little one, being nice to all her family, and keeping all our friends entertained. I realise that the one group I've kind of just left to it are the kids out the back so I go and get some cans and some crisps and take them out, and the older ones get on my case about going on the bouncy castle. Then a few of my mates come out and they join in, so finally I give in and take my shoes and jacket off while the little kids are cleared off. Apparently the challenge is to for me to do a proper somersault. I get on, bounce up and down a couple of times, and then I go for it. As I hit the deck I hear this ripping noise, and my first instinct is I've hurt myself, but then I hear everyone laughing as I climb to my feet, and it's then I realise I've split my trousers, basically all the way along my crack. From the belt loop at the top all the way round to the bottom of my zipper. Thank God I'm wearing clean underwear is my first thought! Everyone is pissing themselves laughing, and at the end of the day it's only a pair of trousers, so I bend over so my backside is facing everyone and slap my arse cheeks. Just as the back door to the pub opens. Just as Alison voice says, 'Stan is just out here, Auntie. I cannot wait for you to meet him.' Just as everyone else basically legs it and leaves me to face not just the wrath of the wife, but the face, the arrogant face, the looking-down-her-nose-at-me face of her aunt. Every ounce of effort I've put into the day dissolves in an instant. It wasn't the split trousers she was annoyed about. It really wasn't. It was that I'd given her aunt the satisfaction of being smug. And of course my involvement in the planning for any future events includes the line 'Well yes, dear, but no bouncy castle this time.' Like I'd be that stupid twice."

His wife, Alison, deigns to disagree. She shakes her head in a way that suggests a deep rooted fatigue, that she has seen this type of thing one time too many. That she expects nothing but the worst from her man.

Alison, 26, Full Time Mum, Salford.

"He's done the same thing twice more since. Fair enough, he wasn't on a bouncy castle but a kid's slide and climbing a fence to get a football back are not exactly the behaviours of a grown up, are they? Let's face it, he's little more than a fool sometimes."

It would appear that the mantra to take on board is split your trousers once, shame on you. Split them twice, shame on you, too, because you must be a massive idiot not to have learnt from the first time. Split them three times? Let's be honest, even the men reading this may have lost sympathy with Stan at that point. Stan's 'Triple Crown' of mistakes at least appears to have been spread out over a number of events possibly stretching to months apart. What if the 'Triple Crown' is achieved within a five minute period? How much trouble would a man expect to be in if that was to happen? Simply, a lot. As much as you can imagine. And then a little bit more. Especially if it's in front of a bunch of your friends.

Kath, 35, Sales Person, Kidderminster.

"We were at our friends' wedding. It has been a great day and even though Adrian got a little bit more drunk than I would have liked or he promised, I didn't mind, really. The next morning we came down to breakfast at the hotel and were sat at a table with my two best friends and their husbands. One of the guys commented to Adrian that he looked a bit ropey, and he confessed that he felt a lot worse than he looked. I was being judgemental when I said to him that I hadn't thought he'd drunk that much. And then he casually confesses that he'd brought a bottle of vodka with him to the wedding and had been sneaking up to our room to top up his drink throughout the night. There was a nervous laugh around the breakfast table and I just knew that everyone was thinking that my husband was pretty cheap. Then the waitress comes and asks for everyone's order. The lads all order the full breakfast. Bacon, sausage, eggs, beans, mushrooms, toast and black pudding. When my girlfriends order their egg and toast or bacon and sausage, or whatever it was that they got, their husband's asked them to order black pudding too, obviously for them. I cannot stand the stuff, so when Adrian suggests I do the same I quietly refuse. Instead of leaving it, though, he starts to make a big deal about it, tried to make out that I'm being a complete and utter bitch. 'I don't even want it to touch my plate,' I mistakenly hiss, my exasperation taking over me. The waitress is uncomfortable, my friends are uncomfortable, I'm starting to fume because now it looks like he's being even more cheap. I know the other guys asked for the same from their wives, but him asking for it on top of the vodka in the room? Finally I give in because this is just embarrassing, and then he leans back in his chair, as smug as can be and he links the fingers of his hands behind his head and he gives me this really arrogant look, and then I can see the state of his shirt under his armpits. It's a light blue shirt but with the sweat stains he has dark blue patches under each arm. Everyone sees. They couldn't miss it. 'Put your arms down.' I snap and I make a face that basically asked what the Hell was going on, and he says in this stupid voice that he'd only worn it once. Once, yes, but that once was all day through a wedding and the evening reception! And yet he thought there was nothing wrong with it. By this point, everyone else was busy examining their cutlery because they were too embarrassed to look up. I've never felt so belittled in my life. A simple breakfast and he manages to do three things at the table that ruin the weekend for me because all I can think about when I remember that weekend is that my friends now think my husband is an oaf. And the worst part of it? I actually agree with them!"

Adrian may argue that his misdemeanours are more to do with Kath's interpretation of his behaviour and how it would make other people think than it was about what he actually did. However, there is definitely a cumulative effect when we men make our mistakes. The first one may be the biggest but if properly dealt with, appropriate apology issued and good behaviour adhered to for the next few weeks, then it can be forgotten relatively quickly. If, however, we follow up the big mistake with two minor errors, it is more likely that the smaller and seemingly insignificant comment or deed will be the catalyst to the apocalypse. And when it kicks off we should expect the scale of the row to reflect the sum of the causes ten-fold and beyond because, let's not forget, they've been storing up every detail, waiting for just this moment to arrive. Not every woman is like this, though, of course, they are not. But still, it must be remembered that even the most forgiving of women have a breaking point.

Gloria, 68, Retired, Swansea.

"Now what I want to ask you is this, see? Why does he wait until I've just done the Hoovering before he cuts his toenails? And why does he have to do them in the living room? It's disgusting, and no matter how many times I ask him, and he promises not to, he still does it. You know where I found a nail clipping once? On the window sill! It's over five feet away. If I'd have been in the room it would have had my eye out, it would."

Whereas much of what a man does wrong may be down to interpretation, flying pieces of hardened and dead human toe claw are unlikely to lead anywhere but down the dark path. There are times, however, when what a man chooses to do with his time will lead to strife even when he is not actually causing anyone any harm directly.

Carla, 26, Head Chef, Hoylake.

"I swear to God, he wouldn't even bother to leave the house unless he had to. The worst thing I ever agreed to was letting him have Sky Sports. He watches all sorts. It's not just the football but all sorts. All of a sudden he loves rugby, cricket, tennis, camel racing. Fishing! Seriously. Fishing? He recorded some national fishing final and watched it at three in the morning after a night out instead of coming to bed when I was well in the mood. Talk about rejection! And if he's not watching sport then he's playing sport. Now if he actually went out and kicked a football around, I wouldn't mind but, no, he's playing it on his damn Xbox. And if he's not playing FIFA or whatever it is, he's shooting terrorists or Nazis. Mind you, if we're talking about the game he likes to play then I would rather he messed about with video games than do what him and his mates did when we had them and their girlfriends over for dinner. Each time one of the lads went to the toilet, when they came back, the rest of the boys would say, completely in the open 'cock' or 'balls' and whoever it was that had been out would say 'yes, cock' or 'yes, balls' and a point would be given to whoever guessed right. Me and the girls, we had no idea what they were up to until one of them came back, says his thing and I can see he's left his zipper open and there's *something* on display. A bit of skin and, oh God I feel sick, a little bit of hair. And then it hits me. Cock. Balls. They were guessing what the hell the other one was showing a little bit of. Apparently it's called just that. 'Cock and balls.' Disgusting. Why would they show their bits to each other? And worse, they've played it all over the place. Even one night in a restaurant when all the girls were there too. What is with that? How can they even justify it? Ask them and all they do is laugh. But trust me. I've warned him. He does it again and Sky Sports gets cancelled and he can't have the next Xbox FIFA game. I'm bribing him and he's twenty-eight. But who's the really stupid one? Me, cos I said I'd marry him!"

Craig Jones and Siôn James

Girls Just Wanna Have Fun (Not that they'd ever admit to it though)

Yes, yes and thrice yes. We agree. We concur. We submit. Men get it wrong. Fact. The evidence is completely substantiated. We make mistakes. We snatch defeat from the jaws of victory. If it reached (and, yes, we have all tried) we would undoubtedly fuck ourselves. And if guns were legal, most men would be walking around limping from where they had shot themselves in the foot. Time and time and time again.

But are we the only ones who get it wrong? Really? Well it would seem that there are some women out there who are prepared to admit that there have been, on the very rarest of occasions, errors of the female variety. Well, three women who are prepared to admit that they have screwed up. Just once each, of course. Of course, the true pay off comes in the form of the way in which their man reacted to said faux pas. The wrong way. Always and obviously the wrong way. But (score one for manly kind) at least these girls got it wrong first.

Honey, won't give her real name, her age or what she does for a living.

"Okay, okay, I'm going to say this once and once only, once ever, so make sure you keep up, okay? Okay, well my other half, and I'm not even telling you his real name because someone might read this and actually be able to work out who we are, so, my other half, he plays tennis. Takes it very seriously, as do the rest of the team he plays in at the club, and they're really successful. Every year they win a league title or a cup or something, and then they have this big awards night where they get trophies for the club tournament, for any leagues they've won, awards, that kind of thing. Okay, so to him it's a big deal. The biggest night of the year. And fair enough, it is, especially this year. He was club singles champion again, and his team had won three trophies in a national league, so it really was a big deal. Now, the thing is, I hate being the centre of attention and normally so does he, but this is the one night of the year when he thinks he is Roger Bloody Federer and I'm right there on his arm, being the perfect little wife. So what do I do to deal with being in the limelight? I drink. Me and one of the other 'tennis widows' get right on the white wine. I forgot to say, we're staying over at his mate's house, and it's the mate's wife and me who are getting wasted. But we're not realising just how wasted we're getting. There's food, there's dancing, and there's the trophies being given out, so the night seems to last for ages, and we get through five, maybe six bottles of wine. Turns out we were only there for three and a half hours. So by the time we get back to their place, the world is spinning and I just want to go to bed. Turns out we are the first guests to stay in their new loft conversion. Where the carpet is new, where all the furniture is new. Where the new fitted bathroom is, you've guessed it, new! So I crash straight out and the next thing I know is that he's out of bed, on the floor on his hands and knees and he's scrubbing the carpet and there's this horrible smell like sick. And my face feels all sticky and when I put my fingers to my cheek and pull them away I see my cheek is covered in sick, and I suddenly have a flashback and I see myself puking in the bed, on the floor, into the sink. Oh my God. And then I must have flaked out again and left him to clean it all up. Which he does like a hero. He even gets me a glass of water and promises he'll never say a word. Until breakfast the next morning when he gets accused of being the one who puked because they heard every single heave and hurl and he grassed me up! I've never wanted to get out of anywhere so fast in my life! Okay, so we finally get home, and the car journey has messed me up, and I end up with my head down the toilet, at least this time I got to the loo, and the phone goes, and it's one of his other mates, and word has spread like wildfire, and the whole tennis club knows, and I'm just thinking how am I ever going to make this up to him when he handed me back the lead with a double fault. 'Yeah, she's on her hands and knees now,' I hear him tell his mate. 'Yeah,' he continues, 'I'm gonna take full advantage. I'm gonna watch the footy'. Game, set and match me!"

Anyone can have the occasional night of nerves where they drink too much. It's allowed. As long as they don't become a menace to themselves or society then usually no long term harm comes of it. Such drunken behaviour in a lady is not the norm, for sure, but it's not like you'd find a female urinating in public, now would you? Would you? Umm, well if you've ever met our next confessor then you would have found a female who urinates in the street. And falls over while doing so. This is her story. Please. Do not judge.

Louise, 31, Lab Assistant, Derby.

"We'd been for a lovely walk through the woods, really, really nice. Ashley had even given up watching some sort of sport so we could go, and he drove, and although we didn't end up where I'd first suggested, his idea was even better. The only difference was that the walk I'd wanted to take would have started at the visitors' centre but his didn't. No biggie. Not to start with. The thing is, there's a toilet at the visitors' centre. There wasn't one where Ashley'd parked. So you can guess the next bit, right? We're halfway back to the car and I'm nearly bursting. We're kind of off the beaten track, and Ashley suggests that maybe I just go behind a bush. He'll keep watch, he says. So I think, what the heck, why not and I go behind this tree where there are some bushes and I drop my jeans, my knickers and squat down. Just as I start, you know, to go, I realise I'm on a bit of a slope, and this takes me from being totally balanced to nearly toppling over backwards. All the while, I'm peeing, mind you, and I start my arms off in big forward swings and there's no chance of me saving myself, and I shout out for Ashley, and as he comes running around the tree over I go backwards. I must have rollie-pollied three, four times, still peeing, so it's going on the floor, up in the air, on the floor, up in the air, and of course, every time it's going up in the air it's like I'm being squirted in the face with a water pistol, and I can hear Ashley running after me, and I must look like a urinating Catherine Wheel, and then I crash through another bush, and I come to rest in the middle of a path that was obviously parallel to the one we'd been on, just a bit lower down the mountain, and while the one we'd been on had been our private track, this one had a mum, a dad, their two kids on bikes and their family dog on it. They all turn and stare at me. The dad is grinning. The mum is horrified. The kids nearly fall off their bikes and the dog trots over and licks me face. Once. Then Ashley crashes through the undergrowth, twenty seconds too late. Now he could save the situation. He could be considerate. He could be thoughtful. Could. Could but, of course, he does not! 'Come on, my dear,' he says. 'Let's get you back to the home.' Even the dog nodded with understanding as the family made their rapid departure away from the very special lady who has no pants on! I couldn't wait to give my lovely thoughtful man a little kiss to thank him."

Now these two confessions left us a little speechless. We were expecting something a little tamer, perhaps something a little bit more expected, more stereotypical. Something to do with driving, perhaps? Well, seeing as you asked... but don't expect a simple prang or putting unleaded in a diesel car. This one will have you, like everyone there, hooting.

Olivia, 26, Accountant, Dublin.

"We all decided we'd go across to Liverpool for a long weekend, but not just to stay in the city and drink, but to actually travel around, so we decided we'd take the car. And then more people got involved so it actually worked out that we'd take two cars. There were four couples in total, so it helped with the cost, and just to make it fun, we decided for travelling over there that we'd have a boys' car and a girls' car. We also decided that each car had to have a theme, like a fancy dress thing just for fun. Well, the boys, they just all wore their Irish rugby jerseys, which was fair enough, but we thought we'd do the whole 'Irish abroad' thing, so the four of us women dressed as Leprechauns. Corny, I know, but it was good fun, and when we parked the car on the ferry and walked up to the bar, everyone was commenting how cool we looked, and we could tell the boys were well annoyed with all of the attention we were getting. So we get to the bar and people are buying us drinks and I'm not drinking cos I'm the driver, for the trip over at least, and Tom, my fella is doing the same. Good tactics see, get the driving out of the way early, and then the rest of the weekend we'd not have to worry. Anyway, the ferry is coming into Liverpool, and the girls have still got all these drinks to finish, so we let the boys head off, down to the car deck while we finish up, and then we look around and we realise we're the only ones left, so we scoop up our bottles and drinks and stuff, and us four Leprechauns amble on down to the car. Well, by the time we get to the car deck half the cars are gone. In fact, it's really easy for us to get to our car cos we're right at the front, and it's really nice cos everyone who's already in their cars is beeping their horns at us, so we wave back and they beep more, hooting away like crazy, and then we see the lads, still sat there in the car behind us and they are cringing and Tom mouths the words 'come on' and signals with his hand for us to hurry, and I think what the Hell is wrong with him, everybody else is being dead nice, and then I look a bit closer at the faces pressed against the car windows, and I suddenly realise that we're not the centre of attention cos everyone loves our outfits but because we are holding them up. 'Get in the car, now,' I hiss and we clamber in, and then someone somewhere shouts something that sounded a lot like 'Move it, you fat slags,' and that's when I knew the fun Irish girls tag had gone right over the side. I look in the rearview mirror and mouth 'I am so sorry,' to Tom, and he's not even looking at me, and I clock that the lads have even taken off their Irish shirts to make sure they weren't associated with us. I know right then that us girls are going to have to work hard to put this right. So I put the car in gear, rev the engine, lift the clutch, and we don't move anywhere because I've left the handbrake on, and that's when Tom drove right into the back of us. We were still on that ferry two hours later."

Tom, 30, So close to being in the right, Dublin.

"Fuck off. Fuck right off."

So although we have limited evidence that women can, in fact, get it wrong just like a man, that evidence is limited. It does, however, offer one crumb of comfort for every man who has made a mistake in their love life. Each and every woman has the potential at least to screw up, and the woman you are with right now, the one who is hogging the Kindle, has most likely done something she is ashamed of since you've been together. She's unleashed a fart that you knew wasn't really the cat. She's spilt food down her best dress. She's insulted your boss at the Christmas dinner. Unfortunately, you've probably managed to overshadow her mistake within a two-minute period. In a ridiculous fashion. Like shitting in your pants. Because you just don't know when you've got it made. But don't blame yourself. None of us do.

And we're still different.

So, as we approach the conclusion of our little guide, we can hear the dissenting voices advancing from the back of your minds to the very tip of your tongues.

"How do I make sure I never make those mistakes again?" the male voices are on the verge of screaming.

"You haven't told us anything we don't already know!" holler the ladies. "You had them at hello! They'd have changed, they'd have listened to you!"

There are two things that the ladies should, however, remember at this juncture. The first is that they never set out to help, change or improve their man. The title is not 'A Man's Guide to Getting it Right.' That would have been a whole different publication and one that we don't think would have been *that* entertaining. Who wants to read anecdotes of charming, handsome men who sweep their loved ones off their feet with style, class and decorum? Who wants to hear tales of the non-existent perfect man who would obviously be played by Colin Firth in the movie version? Face facts, it would only make you feel worse about the man you've chosen to live your life with because he just ain't going to measure up. Wouldn't you rather be reassured at least that your fella isn't the only one with a penis, pooh and pee fetish? That you're not the only woman whose driving gets slated before she even reverses out of the driveway? That he's not the only man who eats at fancy restaurants without using the cutlery?

And the second thing. If you can get over the disappointment of the first, that is? The second thing is that you love your man *despite* of all of the stupid things he's done, is doing right now, and will do in the future. And that gentlemen, is our saving grace. No matter how daft we may be, no matter how far we push things, no matter what we do, they still love us anyway. They know we're never going to change, improve or grow up, and yet they love us anyway. And, lucky for us, loving our wife, fiancée, girlfriend or partner back is the one thing, at least, that a man simply *cannot* get wrong.

The last word on the matter, of course, can come from only one person:

Gloria, 68, Retired, Swansea.

"I knows he's a daft bugger, see, of course I do. You don't live with someone for as long as we have without a little bit of compromise. But he's worth it, he is. Of course he is. Cos I loves him, see."

END!

Craig Jones and Siôn James

About the Authors

Craig Jones has held a wide range of jobs, from tennis coach to gym manager to health service worker. He refuses to admit he's getting older, so please don't tell him, or anyone else. He's had five novels and a bunch of short stories published in the horror genre, but his latest novel falls on the other side of the spectrum, comedy. He lives in beautiful west Wales with his wife Claire, son Shane and a crazy ginger cat, Wookie.

Siôn James: Out the dying embers of a power-pop musical career that found Siôn local celebratory status as part of the best unsigned band to have hailed from the village in which he hails, Siôn took to the written word rather than the lyrical to tell of tales less than ordinary and akin to American Pie meets Bridget Jones. Now a Husband and Father of two, Siôn regales with happenings of floundering nostalgia by way of offering an apology through humour to those who just happened to be in the wrong place, at the wrong time with the wrong person – that being Siôn himself.

More stories from Craig Jones

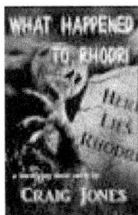 What Happened to Rhodri
(TWB Press, 2011)
A horror short story by Craig Jones

 Gem, the novel
(TWB Press, 2012)
A vampire novel by Craig Jones

 Meat Coma
(TWB Press, 2013)
A zombie short story by Craig Jones

Find more short stories and novels at

TWB PRESS

www.twbpress.com